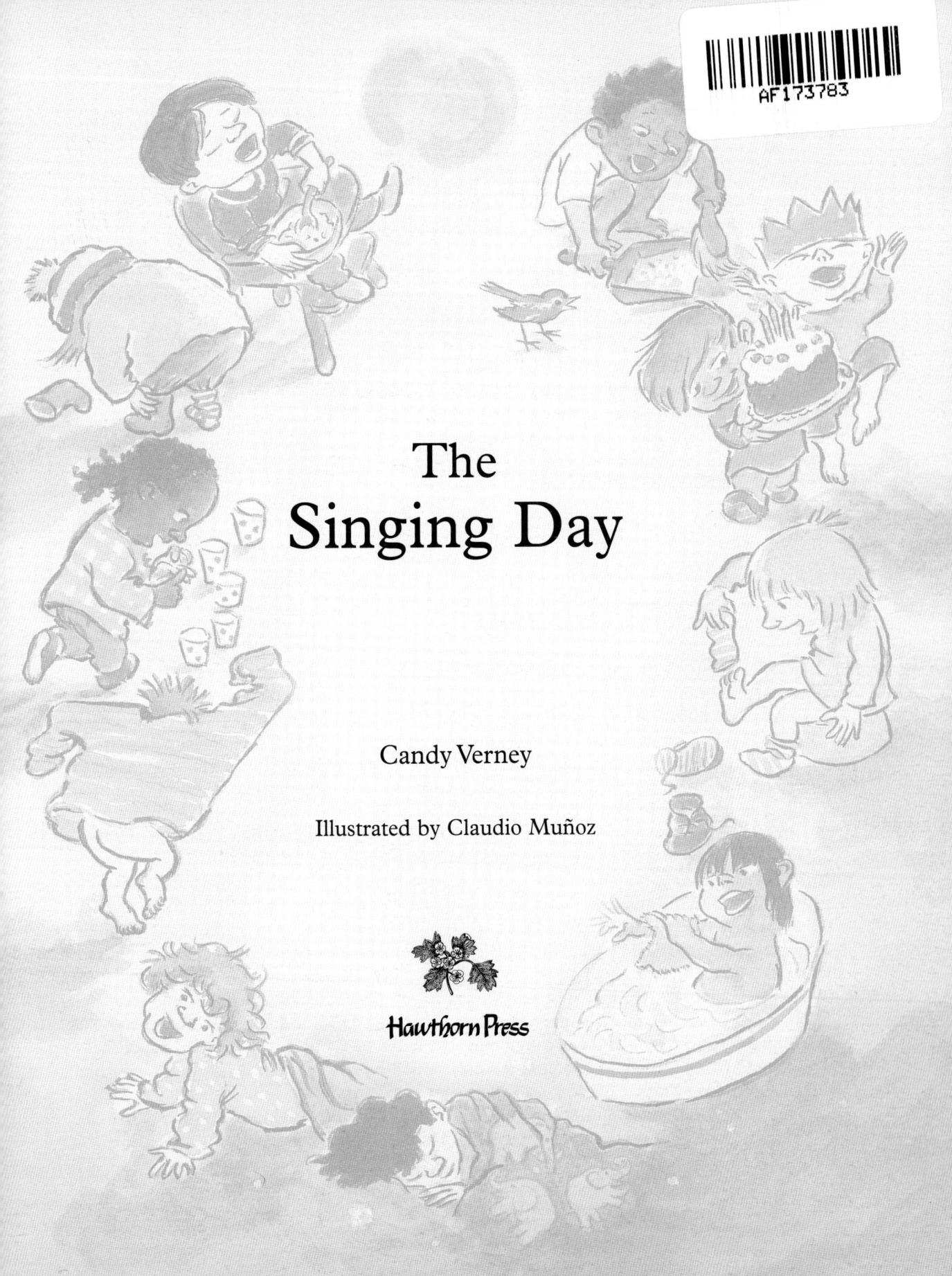

The
Singing Day

Candy Verney

Illustrated by Claudio Muñoz

Hawthorn Press

Published by Hawthorn Press, 1 Lansdown Lane, Stroud, Glos. GL5 1BJ, UK
Tel: (01453) 757040 Fax: (01453) 751138
E-mail: info@hawthornpress.com Website: **www.hawthornpress.com**

Drawings and cover illustration © Claudio Muñoz
Cover design and typesetting by Hawthorn Press, Stroud, Glos.
Additional illustrations by Sarah Fineran and Hawthorn Press
Printed in Europe at the Alden Group, Oxfordshire
Reprinted 2008
CD recorded at DB Studios, Stroud, Glos.

Every effort has been made to trace the ownership of all copyrighted material and to acknowledge this. If any omission has been made, please bring this to the attention of the publisher so that proper acknowledgement can be made in future editions.

The way to Fairyland, Getting up, Lilian McCrae, The policeman walks with heavy tread, E M Adams, Every Thursday morning, Clive Sansom, How many days has my baby to play, anon., In the evening, Ivy O Eastwick from *Book of a Thousand Poems* reprinted by permission of HarperCollins Publishers Ltd. 3 Little Puffins, Trot along my little pony from *Sing through the Day*, Marlys Swinger, 1968 reprinted by kind permission of Plough Publishing House. Daisies, Go to sleep, Joyful greetings, For the golden corn from *Singing through the Seasons*, Marlys Swinger, 1972 reprinted by kind permission of Plough Publishing House. Brush hair, brush from *Pentatonic Songs*, Elisabeth Lebret reprinted by kind permission of Waldorf Association of Ontario. Cha bhi mi 'gad thaladh from *Folksongs and Folklore of South Uist*, Margaret Fay Shaw, 1999 reprinted by kind permission of Berlinn Ltd. Night is here from *The Lullaby Treasury*, Mathilde Polee and Petra Rosenberg, 1997 reprinted by kind permission of Floris Books. Early in the morning, Good morning dear Earth from *Gateways: Poems, Songs and Stories for Young Children*, 1999 reprinted by kind permission of Wynstones Press. Oh the Lord is good to me, Mix a pancake, When I've said my evening prayers from *Festivals, Family and Food*, Diana Carey and Judy Large, 1982 reprinted by kind permission of Hawthorn Press. Extract on page xvi © Iona and Peter Opie 1955. Reprinted from *The Oxford Nursery Rhyme Book* assembled by Iona and Peter Opie (1955) by permission of Oxford University Press. O God guide me, God sufficeth all things above all things by kind permission of the Bahai community. Nellie Bly by Caroline Curtis Brown, published 1927 by Gerald Howe Ltd. Mexican counting song from *Sing a song of sixpence*, Jane Hart and Anita Lobel, 1988 Highland Music Company – all efforts to trace copyright were unsuccessful. Up the wooden hill to Bedfordshire (Connelly/Grey) Campbell and Connelly by kind permission of Music Sales Ltd. Extract on page xiv by kind permission of HarperCollins Publishers Ltd, *Pip Pip, A sideways look at time* © 1999 Jay Griffiths.

British Library Cataloguing in Publication Data applied for.
ISBN 978-1-903458-25-9

Contents

Acknowledgements

When I was first asked to write this book I knew that I wanted to draw on the experience of others: what did they remember of singing from their childhood and how significant a part did it play in bringing up their own children? I visited nursery schools and old peoples' day centres, listening to the songs they sang, and I sent out a circular letter to a wide variety of friends and colleagues asking for their contributions.

I had a wonderful response and I would like to thank everyone who contributed with songs, stories and memories as well as the Opies for their marvellous collection published by Oxford University Press. I am left with a sense of awe at the deep impression music makes on the very young. It can be a marvellous tool to calm the hectic pace of modern family life and it remains an enduring memory and solace in old age. If I have missed anyone out from the list below, please accept my apologies.

I would also like to thank Rachel Jenkins and Martin Large of Hawthorn Press for originally asking me to write this book, and my editor Matthew Barton for his patient and friendly support. Also for the good-humoured vocal contributions of Peter Creed, Claire Atkins and Chris Samuel – grateful thanks indeed. Finally thanks to my good friend Claudio Muñoz for enriching it with his beautiful illustrations.

Contributors:

Aileen Taylor
Alison Hall
Amanda Relph
Anna Glasbrook
Annette Little
Brenda Davies
Bridget Holmes
Carolyn Pellow
Celia Bradshaw
Cindy Mann
Colin & Maggie Smith
Dr. Jean Brown
Elisabeth Marshall
Elizabeth Jackson
Esther Lincoln
Eva Theophile
Hilary Martin
Jane Blackmoor
Jane Darlow
Jean Chancellor
Jean Lynch
Jenni Godwin
Jenny Drake
Jill Newsome

John & Ursula Brooke
Joy de Berker
Judith Verity
Julia Hyde Grossman
Julie Harding
Julie Hewson
Juliet Grainger
Juliet Verney
Katerina Eisch
Ko Hawkes
Linda Webber
Lucy Gaskell
Lucy Metcalfe
Lyoba Jence
Margie Bickford-Smith
Margreth Pfunder-Sonn
Marion Green
Masami Cobley
Matilda Luetchford
Norma Middleton
Olu Oni
Patrick & Anna McCarron
Penny Willis
Peter Creed
Prue Musgrave

Rachel Campbell
Rebecca Reid
Rob Henley
Rose Verney
Sarah Davies
Sebastian Verney
Sheila Macbeth
Sonia Nicholson
Sue Dawkin
Sue Wade
Sulia Rose
Susan Amor
Susan Hicklin
Susan Lacroix
Suzanne Wise
Suzy Pritchard
Terence Molloy
Teresa Harris
Tricia McCleod
Ursula Mommins
Verona Bass
Vicki Knapp
Viv Cole
Viv Talbot

Dedication

To my mother,

who sang me my first song

Foreword

In bygone days, when everyone sang in church on Sunday, when the ploughboy whistled as he walked the fields and Auntie played the piano for a sing-song at family gatherings, live music was very much part of people's lives. Even in the world I grew up in, it was not unusual to hear women singing as they pegged out their washing, and the whistling of the postman was as common as songs on the radio. Consider for a moment what a young child might hear today: breakfast television and music from adverts, snatches of bass line and drums bursting through the windows of passing cars, saxophone music pervading the supermarket aisles and the stylised, digitally-perfected singing of pop-idols.

All these things have their place in our society, but what has happened to our singing? I have become more and more aware, during my years of working with teenagers, that natural singing is sadly missing from many people's lives. Almost all teenagers who sing in choirs with me are those who have early memories of people singing with them and around them when they were small; singing was a normal part of their childhood and it still gives them joy. The more they sing, the more they are able to stand upright and look the world in the eye, and the more confidence they feel in themselves – a confidence which extends far beyond their singing activities.

In this excellent book, Candy Verney explains why it is so important to sing with young children, and explores the many ways in which it can contribute to their healthy development. She opens our eyes to all the opportunities for singing that arise in a child's day, and gives every encouragement, as well as practical tips, to those who are not yet confident enough to start to sing.

Most parents want to give their children some sort of musical education, and most people who are involved in early education recognise that singing can play an important role in this. It is good to know that you don't have to buy expensive musical toys, or provide toddlers with keyboard lessons, or even play them a never-ending stream of recorded music – they will discover all these things as teenagers anyway. By far the most effective way to give children a good start in music – a gift that will last all their lives – is simply to sing with them, right from the start!

Caroline Price
Choir Leader, Stream of Sound Youth Choir

Introduction

I think that nursery rhymes are so deeply entrenched in our history that they speak to children. You cannot sing Twinkle, Twinkle Little Star, *or* Away in a Manger, *without the children loving it. You see their faces open up to that, and it obviously speaks far more deeply to them than we can ever imagine. I don't think we grown-ups have the consciousness left to realise how strong it is…*

What singing means to me

I have always loved songs. From my teenage years onwards I found myself collecting ditties, folk songs and skipping games whenever they came my way. But it was not until I had children of my own that I realised their practical potential. Lullabies – what a lovely, lulling word – soon showed me they held the magical power to soothe a crying child to sleep.

When my first child was born I would anxiously get up in the night so that he did not have to cry for more than a few seconds. Feeding him and trying to get him back to sleep exhausted me. For my third baby, a friend lent me a cradle with a stand which swung on hinges. Suddenly, all I had to do was lean, half asleep, out of my bed, rock the cradle, and the baby would drop off to sleep again. The rhythm of the rocking did the job for me. Why hadn't someone told me about this sooner I wondered? Why did cradles ever go out of fashion? So simple – just the rhythm of rocking calmed the child.

A few years later, one winter's evening, bedtime for my three children, all under five years old, was long overdue. But they were wound up like cars on a racetrack. The higher the emotional temperature rose, the more tired they became. I felt close to breaking point, about to lose my temper, when I remembered a game that my father used to play with us around the dinner table. He would sit in the space between the table and the wall, swinging his arm rhythmically, side to side, as we children ran around the table, taking turns to get through the gap without his arm touching us. I still remember the beating of my heart and my excitement: would I get caught, would I get through? Then the moment of enlightenment when I realised that I could slip past by keeping in time with the rhythm of his arm. I never got caught again!

On that damp November evening, as a creative alternative to losing my temper and spoiling our evening, it came into my mind to try this game, and see if it would calm them down. Spontaneously, I put the movement to a little rhyme, sung to the tune of *The Grand Old Duke of York*:

> *O a-hunting we will go*
> *Across the fields of snow*
> *We'll catch a fox and put him in the box*
> *And then we'll let him go.*

I sat on a child's seat in their bedroom and swung my arm to and fro in the gap between my chair and the bunk beds. As if by magic, the children joined in the game. Each time I caught one of them, I took off a piece of their clothing. Before long, to my amazement, they were tucked up in bed, ready for a story, without trouble or conflict; the job of undressing had been transformed from a chore to a much-loved game that we continued to play for years. In fact, when I recently asked my sixteen-year-old son if he remembered any songs from his childhood, his face lit up immediately. 'Yes, you know, that fox one!'

Song builds up inner resources in children. The lifelong value of this was brought home to me as I researched this book. In the process of collecting songs I have received replies from people up to the age of ninety, who remember the songs sung to them when they were very little children: not only the tunes, but all the verses as well. They were given a treasure chest as children that has served them for the rest of their lives, into which they can dip at any time. One old lady, now nearly blind, deaf, and immobilised, responded when I commiserated with her: 'Oh, I can lie here and recite all my poems to myself.' She has retained an immense repertoire of poetry, first taught to her as a child in Ireland.

Sadly, many of us today have been brought up with very few rhymes, poems or songs. Singing as part of family life is rare – even singing in schools can no longer be taken for granted. But children only need to hear the smallest ditty twice for them to eagerly ask for it again, encouraging you to sing to them. They imitate as easily as breathing. They will readily join in, helping to fill their own inner treasure chest.

As a child, journeys to the seaside with my family seemed endlessly long. We often sang the well-known Harry Belafonte song, *There's a hole in my bucket, dear Lisa, dear Lisa* in which my father would take the lead with obvious pleasure. It wasn't often that we heard him sing, and it managed to break the monotony of that tedious journey. I've liked that song ever since.

My mother would sing arias from her favourite operas around the house. As self-conscious teenagers we teased her about this

habit, but with hindsight it gave us all a lifelong love of music. She also had a way of reading nursery rhymes and little children's stories, slowly and rhythmically, yet with music and playfulness in her voice. The singsong rhythm had a soothing effect on me. I found it immediately reassuring, as if we were both cocooned in a dream world that for a few minutes replaced everyday reality.

A parental resource

Singing can be of immense help to parents in the long haul of everyday routine. It lightens the atmosphere between grown-up and child, can transform a situation from drudgery into playfulness, and also ease the transition from one activity to the next. *Whatever you feel about the quality of your voice, the most important thing from the child's point of view is that you sing.* (See below for help with developing more confidence in singing.) You should feel free to make up your own version of a song to suit each occasion. Nursery songs are part of a wise and generous folk tradition, a body of literature and tunes that expands organically and evolves to suit each generation.

Singing and our global community

As well as rooting a child within his[1] own culture, singing also has a valuable part to play in fostering an appreciation of other cultures and awakening children to the wider human world, to its diversity and richness. Here is a song that was taught to me when I was a little girl:

The little German girl goes Eins, zwei, drei..
The little French girl goes Un, deux, trois…

---

[1] To avoid the awkward use of both genders I will alternate between masculine and feminine forms.

I was intrigued to think that there were children in other places who said those strange words! Singing a song can open a window into that other culture. With this in mind, I have included a few songs in other languages.

Likewise, when a child is involved in a ring game, he is partaking of an activity that has gone on throughout the world since ancient times. The themes of courtship, marriage, war and celebration represent archetypal human activities. By dancing and singing together, we connect to what is universal, and we are reaffirming our union in a common humanity and our place on this unique planet.

The practice of music is our legacy and heritage – perhaps the oldest and most sacred of our musical traditions. Born of an awareness that in some way music-making made us feel bolder and less afraid, music was a vehicle through which we expressed the interconnectedness of our pulsing universe and the unity of its rhythmic cycles long before we were able to give verbal expression to the concepts that were beginning to take shape in our minds. And in that experience of union is music's primary value as a healing force. Overcoming the anxiety of separateness in a world so often perceived as hostile, music is the reassurance of the harmony and purposefulness, the essential order and beneficence of the universe.

RANDALL MCCLELLAN
The Healing Power of Music

Singing with children in the early years

All appeared new, and strange at first, inexpressibly rare and delightful and beautiful. I was a little stranger, which at my entrance into the world was saluted and surrounded with innumerable joys. My knowledge was Divine...

THOMAS TRAHERNE

There are so many reasons for singing with children from the very beginning of their lives (this book focuses particularly on the first three or four years). Above all, they delight in it. They will dance and sing spontaneously when they are happy – a sure sign of their well-being. This was brought home to me clearly once when some neighbours of mine, experienced foster parents, adopted three little sisters. On a visit to their household a few months after the children had arrived, I saw the four-year-old meandering around the garden, in her own world, singing away to herself, clearly showing she had settled into her new home and was happy.

Besides pure joy in singing, there are also developmental and educational reasons which make singing an essential activity in these early years.

Singing development in infants

From their earliest beginnings inside the womb, babies respond to music (see page 89). As early as three months they start moving to music, rhythmically swaying or bouncing. The existence of games for babies throughout the world – foot play, finger play, Peek-a-boo – are testimony to children's love of and need for such structured movement.

Toddlers will dance as soon as they can stand up. At about eight months, after the babbling stage, their first songs are often wonderfully inventive, using snatches of songs they have heard and mixing them with their own repertoire of words and phrases. Psychologists call these 'outline songs'. Though they are not exact imitations of known songs, they follow the gist or the contour of a song. This is a form of dreamy musical play, and a necessary stage of development in preparation for other forms of music making. These early experimentations represent children's self-activity, the roots of their life-long creativity. They are mastering their native music, making it their own, and expressing their own inner state at the same time.

Parents and primary carers naturally talk to their infants from birth in a way particularly suited to their child. Psychologists have called this verbal interaction 'motherese'. Often the infant initiates this and the adult responds. This form of communication between adult and infant exists universally across cultures and plays a major role in babies' speech and singing development.

It is amazing that mothers throughout the world use similar or identical melodic phrases to communicate similar emotions such as approval, warning, soothing and love.

From my experience of remedial work with adults unable to hold a melody when singing, I believe that 'non-singers' had no one in their early years who sang and spoke 'motherese' to them. As a result their voices never learnt to imitate tunes, to 'fine-tune' themselves. Singing to children helps the voice find and orientate itself, helps voice and ear co-operate in reproducing a tune.

It is important not to censor, correct or hurry these early stages. Children vary enormously in their capacity and speed when learning to sing 'in tune' as adults would define it. Some sing beautifully before they are one, others only learn at eight or nine, and then only if given some help with conscious listening. It does not mean they are 'unmusical', and real damage may be done to both voice and self-esteem if corrections are made too early, or in a critical manner.

My early experiences of singing were that my mother had perfect pitch; so if I sang she would *correct the notes and tell me that I was doing it wrong. As a result, I have always felt that I couldn't sing.*

It is worth noting that our judgement of what is 'in tune' or not is culturally specific. The underlying scale (or series of notes) we use in the modern western world is only one of many that have developed in other cultures over the centuries. What sounds in tune for us will sound out of tune to others around the world, whose music is based on a different tuning system. Our western contemporary tuning (for instance on the piano) is a contrivance that came into use in the 18th century, when some intervals were compressed to make them fit into a system, so-called equal temperament. While most adults have learnt to sing these intervals, the small child will not, because her organ of hearing has not yet adapted to our cultural confines.

Singing and movement as aids to other learning

In addition to purely musical development, singing and movement are central to many other areas of children's learning. Piaget first identified the time between 0-3 years as the 'sensory-motor' stage of development, meaning that sensation and movement are the primary way in which children learn about themselves and their environment. Children at this age need to run, jump, skip, tumble, roll and be vocal. They are co-ordinating their muscles, learning about balance, training their memories, which they need to do sufficiently before they can be asked to sit still and learn in a conventional way.

In the field of memory, a child learns the skills of reading, writing, spelling and number after first developing three basic memory skills: visio-spatial, auditory and short-term memory. Music and movement are intrinsic to developing all three.

Visio-spatial skill grows out of the child's knowledge of herself in space, through balancing and movement; auditory memory develops through listening, speaking and singing; and short term memory develops through repetition. As regards word-building, Sally Goddard-Blythe, from the Institute of Neuro-physiological Psychology, Chester, has done extensive research in this field, and describes music as one of the most powerful instruments we have to give children a basic reference library of sounds.[2] A list of other recent studies corroborating these findings are listed in the Bibliography.

One of the greatest music educators of the twentieth century, Zoltan Kodaly, spent a major part of his life researching and promoting the benefits children gain from singing. As a result of his work, the Hungarian government set up a series of music primary schools all over Hungary from 1950 onwards, which were open to children regardless of musical ability. Here, singing and music were part of the daily curriculum. The educational development of children from these schools was compared over a number of years with those in normal state primary schools. The results were dramatic. In addition to an expected increase in musical ability, those in the music primary schools demonstrated a vastly increased capacity in other educational areas:

* ability to memorise
* capacity for reasoning and disciplined thinking
* richness of emotional range in descriptive writing and speaking
* more active participation in school work
* increased ability to learn foreign languages, through better capacity to imitate, concentrate and memorise
* aesthetic awareness and sensitivity to colour, expressed in a greater facility for drawing and painting
* improved development of children's thorax and respiratory organs, and likewise their awareness of breathing

From my own work in primary schools I can corroborate these findings. In a school where music and movement had been deleted from the curriculum for at least two years, due to pressure to improve literacy and numeracy, the children had difficulty moving fluidly, their movements were uncoordinated and awkward, their singing voices largely out of tune, and most children could not stamp or clap in time. The image that came to me as I sang and moved with the children was of pouring water on dry, parched earth.

Kodaly advised that if a child is having difficulty learning the 3 Rs, one should give her more time for singing and movement, and this would help with academic learning.

---

2 In *Music and Movement* (page 7), Sally Goddard-Blythe writes: 'The process of vocalising sounds to music builds up a storehouse of vocabulary, or lexicon, which may be called upon at any time. The process of putting words to music, and of pointing, naturally breaks words down into separate syllables by giving one or several notes for each unit of sound within the word, placing emphasis on key consonants and slowing down the sounds of speech, so that every phoneme within a word is articulated. In this way, not only is the voice trained, but also the ear, the eye and memory.'

A word about rhythm and repetition

Children live in the heart of the ocean of time itself, in an everlasting now. A child's eternal present is present-absorbed, present-spontaneous, present-elastic.

JAY GRIFFITHS
Pip, Pip, A Sideways look at time

Rhythm is very important in young children's lives. Not so much the mechanical beat of the metronome, but the movement of the breath, contraction and expansion like the sea's tide flowing in and out. Children have no use for, and no conception of linear time, but they thrive when their day has a breathing rhythm, a flow between the IN of peace, rest, reflection; and the OUT of activity, action and interest in the world.

When such rhythm becomes a part of the child's everyday experience, it promotes health and contentment, and strengthens growing life forces. The world is chaotic without rhythm. Singing can be used as signposts and cornerstones to mark these flowing rhythms: not only of the day, but also the longer rhythms of the week, and to celebrate the annual rhythms of the seasons and the cycle of the year.

This volume focuses on daily rhythms, while the companion volume *The Singing Year,* encompasses the larger sweep of the seasons, with their own greater in- and outbreath.

A repertoire of songs repeatedly sung at 'tidy up time', or at bedtime, can foster a child's sense of security and build self-confidence. As she grows older, so songs may change to suit differing needs. But some will remain as family favourites.

Rhythm can also enter the way we actually sing songs to little ones. With young children we do not aim for a precise, metronome rhythm that would fit with a drumbeat, but one that reflects a song's words and mood. Sing it liltingly, feeling free to slow down to anticipate some action, speeding up again to reflect the meaning of the words. This is enlivening to young children, as their response will prove.

Here are the observations of two nursery teachers, relating how rhythm helps them in their daily work with children:

Singing to children brings about that transparent quality in them; they're so open to song, and they'll look at you with their shining eyes. We use so much instruction, so much spoken word. But you can use singing to do all the chivvying along, and they will always respond to it so well. In the nursery, a song will be an indication that something's starting or something's ending. It makes transitions so much easier. Children live in a musical element, they live in the music.

SARAH DAVIES
Nursery teacher

Many children today are in situations where they are prematurely woken to a wider world, with its adult preoccupations, expectations and dangers…Their inborn trust is frequently shaken by the inconsistencies in their lives: Is Daddy leaving? Who will pick me up? Where are we going now? … Anxieties can and do gradually ease, however, as the kindergarten's daily and weekly rhythms lift from the child the burden of wondering what will come next, what will be expected of her. The steady, returning rhythms of the kindergarten are particularly healing for children in difficult circumstances. They signal to the child: 'Here you are safe and you can trust in what you'll find.

LYNNE OLDFIELD
in *Free to Learn*

What sort of music?

It is worth giving some thought to the kind of music that we use with young children. Obviously there is tremendous value in nursery rhymes and well-known songs, some of which are included in this collection. When introducing new songs it is also worth bearing in mind that the pentatonic scale is particularly suited to young children.

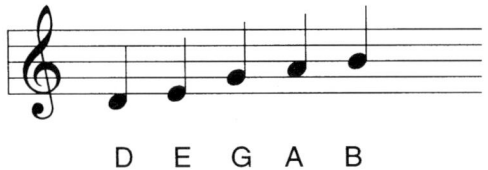

D E G A B

If a child first has a firm grasp of the five 'pillar' tones of the pentatonic scale, he will later find it easy to fit in the half step between them.
KATALIN FORRAI
in *Music Education in Hungary*

This is a scale found in folk music all over the world, and from the most ancient times. Parts of it are used instinctively by children in their games, as in the phrases 'I'm the king of the castle', and 'I'm coming, ready or not'.

It has an innate simplicity, with no semitones in the scale, which makes it easier to sing. It also can float naturally here and there, without a strong pull down to the 'home' note, the tonic, as in our major and minor scales. This reflects where young children are at, in a consciousness of imaginative make-believe, in a world which is dreamy and not yet anchored in more mundane realities or focused tasks.

Some of the songs included in this book are pentatonic. They may sound unfamiliar at first hearing. This is because our adult ears have become conditioned to hearing a predominance of music in major and minor keys. But young children are very happy with them.

A word about recorded versus live music

Although tapes and CDs have their place, there is nothing that equals the value of a child's very own 'live music': that of being sung to. We accept that physical nourishment is vital for the child's growing body, but are less likely to recognise that everything else the child takes in through his senses has a similar effect. Just as children need and thrive on human touch, human response and love, so they need to hear the sound of the human voice. Voice production is a highly complex and finely tuned process. Children need to make complex observations, trials, experiments with their voice, that are learnt from the people around them. It is the direct connection that is important: when a mother sings to her baby, she transmits a range of tones, frequencies, breathing patterns, facial movements and vitality that is impossible to replicate in a tape or CD.

A word of warning

Infants have highly sensitive ears that can be damaged, literally 'de-tuned', by very loud or low frequency sounds. Exposure to loud sounds over extended periods of time will prompt the ear to tune out certain frequencies to protect itself, and as a result, will be less able to listen and learn well. For further reading on this issue, I recommend the work of Dr. Alfred Tomatis (see Bibliography), who has connected auditory damage to many chronic conditions e.g. dyslexia, depression, Attention Deficit Disorder (ADD), and Hyperactivity (ADHD).

Incorporating songs into everyday life

The fact delighted in is the special performance for the strictly limited audience. A mother's own voice is worth more than four-and-twenty professional singers trilling on the radio.
©Iona and Peter Opie

[Reprinted from the *Oxford Nursery Rhyme Book* assembled by Iona and Peter Opie (1955) by permission of Oxford University Press.]

So where do we start? A natural place would be to sing the very familiar nursery rhymes that you probably know from your own childhood:

- Round and round the garden like a teddy bear
- Here we go round the mulberry bush
- Humpty Dumpty

etc.

You will find that they flow easily: part of your own store of memories.

There are several times in the day which lend themselves easily to singing: changing a nappy, mealtimes, bedtime, getting a child undressed. Use a song that you know well, or choose one to learn from this book. Then there are activities with a rhythm in them: swinging, walking down the street, going upstairs. Try to choose a song that has rhythm similar to the activity.

Repetition is very important – children love to hear the same song at a similar point of the day, or accompanying the same activity. They learn songs very quickly and will imitate you (from about two years onwards). Any song that you have taken the trouble to learn by heart they will soon know, and help you remember it if you go wrong!

The wonderful thing about singing at home is that there is no right and wrong way to do it, no copyright laws to worry about, no experts to advise you – you can develop your own personal family repertoire, singing the songs that develop between individual members of your family. It is a wonderful way to nurture family closeness, to develop a shared history, your own family's treasure chest.

All of the above applies to a Day Nursery situation also. This is the child's family for the hours that she is there. Using singing as a form of live punctuation during the day will help the child feel settled in her new environment. It is very important to use the same songs for the same activity. The child will get to know through the singing of the song, that it is time to tidy up, or that it is nearly time for dinner, or that it is quiet time. 'Good morning' songs and 'goodbye' songs will help the child to adapt from home to day care. Singing establishes confidence and a sense of security:

I watch children who haven't had singing in their lives before: they look at you and stare and giggle, they love it so much. They get such joy from it. The repetition in songs is really important as well.
Sarah Davies
Nursery teacher

Accompaniments

Although some song books have piano/guitar accompaniment, and children will enjoy singing along when someone is playing an instrument, the most important thing for younger ones is the direct connection between you and them, not only your attention, but the physical movements that spontaneously happen when you sing with them – the rocking, jiggling, clapping and games.

'Of course I can't make up my own songs...'

Well, yes, of course you can! The spontaneous act of making up a story or song with or for a child is a precious gift to him. High poetry is not needed, but just that attention to the child and creativity in response to him, which he senses directly.

My father used to make up stories for us as children. They centred on a character called Little Mo. I have forgotten the storyline, but I still remember the joy and inner glow that I felt when he related another episode.

You can start with a well known tune like *Here we go round the mulberry bush* and make up the simplest of ditties that express some activity that you do regularly with your child: getting undressed, going upstairs, putting on coats and hats. The child will especially love it if his own name is included. Here are some very simple examples:

'This is the way we water the garden, water the garden, water the garden' etc. (to the tune of *Mulberry Bush)*

'Oh the shopping trolley is full, we'll have to give it a pull.' *(Grand Old Duke of York)*

'Joey's feet are climbing up, one, two, one, two. We're going up the stairs, till we reach the top!' (Sung rhythmically, in time with your steps)

Children not only appreciate your efforts, however timid, but they will copy you, and probably outstrip you in humour and quality.

I asked the mothers of children who had been coming to a toddler singing group for several months what effect the singing had on their children, and whether it affected their family life. Here are some responses:

We were going round a supermarket. Emily was bored, she started singing, making up her own words to familiar tunes about what she could see – e.g. putting the pasta in the basket. When we're out and about, people comment on how happy she seems, as she's always singing to herself.

Maisie was full of excitement in the car one morning, as she had seen a baby lamb on the way. I expressed interest in what she had seen. Then she suddenly said, 'Sing it!' She is used to singing her way through life.

Our singing toddlers group has increased my confidence and stopped me feeling inhibited about singing. It's just part of normal life now. It has given us another easily accessible tool, another strand to my daughter's and my relationship. It's very much around.

When Emily, aged 2½, doesn't want to do something, or I find we need to change activity, I start singing it, e.g. 'We're all going to the shops.' She then becomes keen to do it.

When Isaac was younger and could not yet talk, he used some of the songs and their actions to communicate. For example, he would tell me to stop by bringing his arms down and slapping his knees, an action we had done in the rhyme Roly Poly.

Lily (just 2 years) doesn't sing that much yet, but she recognises all the songs.

'I love music, but I can't sing' – encouragement for reticent singers

Many people describe themselves as being unable to sing. This is an effect of our modern life style. Unless we were very lucky, we did not experience much singing in our childhood. As a result, we never developed the habit, our voices did not get a chance to learn, and our innate confidence drained away.

In former days, singing was a daily activity that accompanied the rhythms of work, whether hammering on an anvil, washing clothes, or pulling in the nets, as well as being a central activity in community entertainment. Children were brought up hearing the adults around them singing, and consequently learned to sing. There are many places in the world where singing still plays a daily part in the celebration of life.

Many 'non-singers' can remember an incident in their childhood when a teacher, a parent or another child made a critical comment about their voice which humiliated them. From then on, sometimes for a lifetime, they have kept quiet. Damaging comments of this kind often come from a misguided belief that singing is a gift you are or are not born with. Children are either 'musical' or not. Even today, in schools, most children are not taught to sing. It is a curious anomaly that we expect to teach children to read and write, but think they should be able to sing without help.

The following comments are by adults who learned how to sing in midlife, and continue to gain immense pleasure from it:

It was just before Christmas and I was 6½ years old. The infants' choir for the nativity play had been chosen. I was not in it but not everyone was. Another of the infants' teachers then

selected a non-choir group to go around the classes singing carols outside the classroom doors. I was the only non-choir member not selected. This is when I knew I could not sing.

As a child I didn't sing; we didn't sing at home and I don't remember singing at school. My parents were always too busy to sing and I grew up with a belief that I was tone deaf, frightened to utter a note in case it was the wrong one. I have always lacked confidence in expressing myself.

In my work I find that most 'non-singers' *can* sing – they can sing in tune and have a sense of rhythm. But they lack confidence. Our feelings of inhibition and embarrassment at singing in company get passed on to our children, and this eventually curtails their natural and spontaneous love of singing and dancing. The wonderful thing is that our young children's delight in these activities and their innate tolerance and trust of us can help us reverse this negative cycle. We only have to try a little, and their enthusiasm will encourage us. Once we have got over initial embarrassment, the child's positive responses will help.

It is also useful to know that there are a number of steps we can take to restore our voice to its natural capacity. There are two main areas to look at – breathing and listening.

Breathing

In a natural and healthy breathing system the body is a relaxed organism, the breath flowing in deeply to the abdomen, then out again. This continues as we sing. Those who feel they cannot copy a tune probably experienced a time in their childhood when a part of their singing apparatus was blocked in some way.

Tensions and constrictions can build up in any one of several areas of the body used in singing: the head, neck and throat, shoulders, chest and abdomen.

Breathing exercise

The Avon Gorge in Bristol is a deep muddy ravine, with the river Avon flowing through it. This immense body of water flows in and out twice a day, rising 30 feet from high to low tide. But the river bed that contains all the water does not move at all.

Imagine your body is the riverbed, and the air you breathe is its tidal water. Lie on your back, head supported and raised a little, so that all your vertebrae are flat on the floor. Raise the knees, hands resting on the stomach, get really comfortable, and breathe normally. Imagine yourself as the river gorge, lying still and relaxed, and your breath like the water flowing in through an open channel, then flowing out again, out, out, out... so that the tide is out completely, there is no water left in the river bed.

Just as the gorge does not *actively* suck the water back, so you *allow* the breath to flow back in by itself, feel yourself opening up, there is no effort involved, until the river is high again. Aim for a state of peace and relaxation. Only the belly gently swells as the breath comes in, and then flattens as the breath goes out – the shoulders, neck and throat should remain relaxed, hardly moving.

Then slowly stand up, keeping the same state of relaxation, shoulders relaxed, no tension in the chest or neck as the breath flows in and out. Now try humming, chanting any note. If this comes easily, try singing a few notes, maybe with someone you trust.

If you can maintain this relaxed and natural breathing state and sing at the same time, you are well on the way to finding your voice.

Listening

There is a difference between hearing and listening. As I sit here at the computer my son is listening to the radio; it is a glorious spring day and the birds are singing outside. For most of the morning I have not heard the birds or the radio. I have been absorbed in my own thought process, writing these words. But the sounds are still travelling along my auditory nerves to my brain. It is my perceptual awareness that changes, enabling me either to listen or not.

If I pause from my work, I can start listening, and the birds and radio will come into my hearing again.

The background level of noise in our urban world does not encourage us to listen. We hear all the sounds around us, but the ear learns to cut off, to protect itself from over-stimulation.

In fact we can improve our singing voice by learning to listen. People who feel unconfident when singing often hear the note, then panic at the thought of having to reproduce it. They rush to sing, as if the speed will somehow get the ordeal over with quickly. But their ears may not have had a chance to listen to the note.

Listening exercises

Work with a trusted friend or teacher:

1. She sings a note.
   You breathe out strongly, then breathe in and try to sing the same note.
   Repeat with the same or other notes, establishing a rhythm between you.

2. She sings a note.
   Listen to the note first, *pause,* sing the note inside your head, then try to reproduce it.

3. Singing while moving is also very helpful. Panic is linked to thoughts. If you move while singing the thought process is kept at bay, so that the natural voice has a chance to come out. Pretend to dig up potatoes as you sing; or march, jump or swing your arms.

As you concentrate on improving your singing voice in these ways – through breathing and listening – your hearing will become more acute. You may start to hear subtleties in sounds that you were unaware of before, e.g. whether a note is higher or lower than its neighbour.

Starting to sing

However you feel about your voice, just try starting with a simple song, maybe a very simple lullaby e.g. *Bye Baby Bunting* (page 69). Learn it off by heart, then sing it to your child.

After two or three times your child will start responding, showing recognition, which will encourage you to carry on. You may find the child is delighted!

If you really feel you cannot keep a tune at all, then try speaking or chanting a rhyme to accompany a daily activity, e.g. *Little man in coal pit* (page 6) while you get him dressed. The child's obvious enjoyment will soon encourage you.

Build up a few rhymes that you and your child enjoy. This will develop your confidence.

Then ask a trusted friend to sing a very simple song with you. You could start with the two notes of *'Shoe a little horse'* (page 39). Sing it over and over again, making sure that they always start on the same note. If that goes well, add an extra note so that you are singing the notes of:

I'm the king of the castle
Get down you dirty rascal

Now you could try some of the songs in this book:

* Ring the bell ('Getting dressed')
* Carrots, potatoes, cabbage and peas ('Food and mealtimes')
* All in a row ('Coming home')
* Bye baby bunting ('Lullabies')

One woman, Sulia, found it hard to pitch notes or to sing high. She recognised a joy for singing in her eldest child and wanted her children not to be blocked as she had been. So she came for singing lessons, and made a tape of songs for them all to learn, herself included. It developed her confidence, and also helped her children learn to sing from her, their dad and the tape. They learned through her enthusiasm and perseverance – and began to tell her when she was out of tune! The children now all sing beautifully and it is a major part of their family life.

There are professional teachers who specialise in helping people find their voice (see 'Organisations' at back of book). Before you sign up for a lesson, check that they work with 'non-singers'. I have never met anyone who could not learn to sing with help. Nor have I met anyone who was 'tone deaf'. See Natural Voice Practitioners' Network to find a teacher.

Helping children sing

Below are some teaching techniques that help children to tune their voices and sing well at a young age:

- Try to start on the same note each time you repeat a song. This is comparable to giving the voice a map to orient itself.
- Sing quite high – children's voices are naturally higher than adults.
- Repetition: children love and need to have songs repeated. I sing each song 2-3 times at a go, especially when I have just introduced it. Then I continue to sing it for many consecutive sessions. Not only do children love the familiarity they gain in this way, but it helps to tune their voices. I gradually introduce other songs and drop the original ones, keeping a balance between familiarity and new interest.
- Sing at a pace that suits the age of the child. Don't sing too fast. Children need time to grasp tunes and accompanying actions.
- Be flexible with the rhythm. I often pause on the first note of a song. This indicates to the children that we are starting, and 'gathers them in'. It also helps their voices to find the note (even adults need this), and brings a playful feeling of anticipation to the music.
- Movement is central to helping children sing in tune and find the rhythm. You can help a child by holding his hand and walking along, singing the song in time with your feet, or bouncing him gently on your knee.
- Children pick up the mood you create. Be playful, enjoy yourself!

And a few final notes...

Finally, a note about the selection of songs: I have included a few very well known nursery songs, but there are many I have left out, for the simple reason that they are readily available elsewhere.

You will notice that when the songs are sung on CD, the singer does not follow the exact rhythm of the notes. This is done deliberately. Bar lines in written music are limiting and mechanical (see section on rhythm): they cannot possibly show all the nuances of music that is alive and fresh. It is this fresh quality which feeds the young child's heart and soul, so don't curtail your natural talents by sticking too rigidly to beat or bar lines. You are in good company – Chopin did it all the time!

Singing rounds

Young children are not likely to be able to hold a tune 'against' others as is necessary in a round. But they can still enjoy the sounds of the harmonies if older children and adults sing rounds.

Songs through the Day

Waking up

Julie and Robert had to be out one day, and they asked me to look after the baby for a couple of hours. When I arrived, Claire was in her cot asleep upstairs. Robert showed me where the milk was and asked me to wake her and feed her at eleven o'clock. I was a bit apprehensive at this, and said, 'Look, this poor baby has never *seen me, and she might scream the place down when I wake her.' However when the time came I thought I would sing to her as I walked up the stairs to wake her gently. She was absolutely delighted and tried to sing along with me. Each time she saw me after this she started singing.*

Morning has come

CD TRACK 1

Mor- ning has come Night is a- way;

Rise with the sun And wel- come the day

Morning has come
Night is away;
Rise with the sun
And welcome the day.

Good morning dear earth
Good morning dear sun
Good morning dear trees and flowers every one.
Good morning, dear beasties
And birds on the tree.
Good morning to you
Good morning to me.

3

Nellie Bly

CD TRACK 2

Nellie Bly shuts her eye,
When she goes to sleep;
And in the morning when she wakes
The frog begins to peep –
Hi, Nellie! Ho, Nellie!
Won't you come with me?
I'll dance for you
I'll sing for you
The sweetest melody.

Early in the morning

MUSIC: CANDY VERNEY

Ear- ly in the morn- ing Oh hear the cock- erel call.   He struts about the

slower

farm- yard 'Good morning, creatures all,'   He   flaps his wings and

sings   to you 'Wake   up   now,   cock -a- dood- le-   doo.'

Early in the morning
Oh hear the cockerel call.
He struts about the farmyard
'Good morning, creatures all,'
He flaps his wings and sings to you
'Wake up now, cock-a-doodle-doo.'

To the tune of *Drunken Sailor*

What shall we do with sleepy Mary?
What shall we do with sleepy Mary?
What shall we do with sleepy Mary?
Early in the morning.

Stroke her cheek and pat her on the shoulder,
Stroke her cheek and pat her on the shoulder,
Stroke her cheek and pat her on the shoulder,
Early in the morning.

Heave ho and UP she rises
Heave ho and UP she rises
Heave ho and UP she rises
Early in the morning.

Other options:

We'll clean her teeth until they sparkle…
We'll put on her pants and vest and T-shirt…

Getting dressed

Rob had problems waking up from his afternoon nap, at about 2 years old. He was very bad tempered. I found it worked to sing our way through getting him ready. I'd make up silly rhymes that would make him laugh. With him on my lap, I'd sing him into his clothes, making up the tune as I went along: 'Here comes that silly old vest, let's put it on.' 'Mr Big Toe is going first…' (to put on socks).

Ring the bell

CD TRACK 4

OXFORD NURSERY RHYME   MUSIC: CANDY VERNEY

Ring the bell, *(tug lock of hair)*
Knock at the door, *(tap forehead)*
Peep in, *(peer into eyes)*
Lift the latch, *(touch nose)*
Walk in. *(open mouth)*
Go way down cellar and eat apples. *(tickle throat)*

Putting on pyjamas, or a sweater:

Little man in the coal pit
Goes knock, knock, knock;
Up he comes, up he comes,
Out at the top.

Scrub your dirty hands

CD TRACK 5

Scrub your dir- ty hands Scrub your dir- ty hands

Scrubba dub dub dub Scrubba dub dub dub Scrub your dir- ty hands.

Scrub your dirty hands
Scrub your dirty hands
Scrubba dub dub dub
Scrubba dub dub dub
Scrub your dirty hands.

Every Thursday morning
Before we're quite awake,
Without the slightest warning
The house begins to shake
With a Biff! Bang!
Biff! Bang! Biff!
It's the dustman, who begins
(Bang! Crash!)
To empty all the bins
Of their rubbish and their ash
With a Biff! Bang!
Biff! Bang! Bash!

CLIVE SANSOM

To the tune of *Mulberry Bush* (see page 102,
CD TRACK 87)
This is the way we clean our teeth...
This is the way we brush our hair...
This is the way we put on our socks...

When I get up in the morning

MUSIC: adapted by
CANDY VERNEY from the English
folk tune *The Lincolnshire Poacher*

WORDS: LILLIAN McCREA

When I get up in the morning
I'll tell you what I do,
I wash my hands and I wash my face,
Splishety-splash, splishety-splash,
I clean my teeth till they're shining white,
Scrubbity-scrub, scrubbity-scrub,
Then I put on my clothes and I brush my hair,
And I runnity-run, I run downstairs.

Brush hair, brush

CD TRACK 7

NURSERY RHYME   MUSIC: E. LEBRET

Brush hair, brush,
The men have gone to plough,
If you want to brush your hair,
Brush your hair now.

Wash hands, wash,
The men have gone to plough,
If you want to wash your hands,
Wash your hands now.

Clean teeth, clean etc.

Changing nappies

We sing any song, but ring the changes or it stops working. 'Round and round the garden' is a favourite.

For several months 'Humpty Dumpty' was the only song Rosanna allowed us to sing.

How many days has my baby to play?

CD TRACK 8

NURSERY RHYME

MUSIC: CANDY VERNEY

How many days has my baby to play?
Saturday, Sunday, Monday,
Tuesday, Wednesday, Thursday, Friday,
Saturday, Sunday, Monday.

Leg over leg as the dog went to Dover, (*cross and uncross baby's legs*)
He came to a stile, JUMP he went over. (*lift child in the air*)

Getting ready to go out

Come Kieran let us go

CD TRACK 9

Come *Kieran* let us go,
Put on your walking shoes,
It's time to move along
So put on your walking shoes.

*This can be adapted for hopping, skipping,
jumping etc.*

On with my coat
And on with my hat
On with my boots that go
Splish splosh splat
On with my gloves
So woolly and warm
And out to the shops
Just me and my mum. (or: With *Jamie* and Mum.)

CANDY VERNEY

11

Coming home

Many parents have told me of rhymes that
they sang to encourage tired children to walk
home. Here are some:

All in a row

CD TRACK 10

All in a row, all in a row (*walk along holding hands with a child on each side*)
Catching a rabbit and shooing a crow (*pull the children together*)
All in a row.

Trot, trot trot

CD TRACK 11

Trot, trot trot,
Go and never stop.
Where 'tis smooth and where 'tis stony,
Trudge along my little pony,
Go on and never stop.
Trot trot trot trot trot.

Horsey, horsey

Horsey,   horsey,   don't you stop,   Just let your feet go   clippety clop.   Your

tail goes swish And the wheels go round,   Gid- dy up we're   homeward bound.

(hold child's hand throughout)
Horsey, horsey, don't you stop, *(walk along, then stop with feet together)*
Just let your feet go clippety clop. *(trot along)*
Your tail goes swish *(lift one leg high in the air)*
And the wheels go round, *(child goes under your arm in a circle)*
Giddy up we're homeward bound. *(hold hands and run forwards)*

---

*If we were walking somewhere, and we were getting bored,
my Dad who had been in the RAF would say:*

Changing step,
On the march
1   2   3   4   *(point toe forward, side, back, forward
then start off again on the other foot.)*

*It amused us, we found it silly and funny. It changed the
atmosphere from being boring to being a bit exciting.*

13

Trot along, my little pony

WORDS AND MUSIC: MARLYS SWINGER

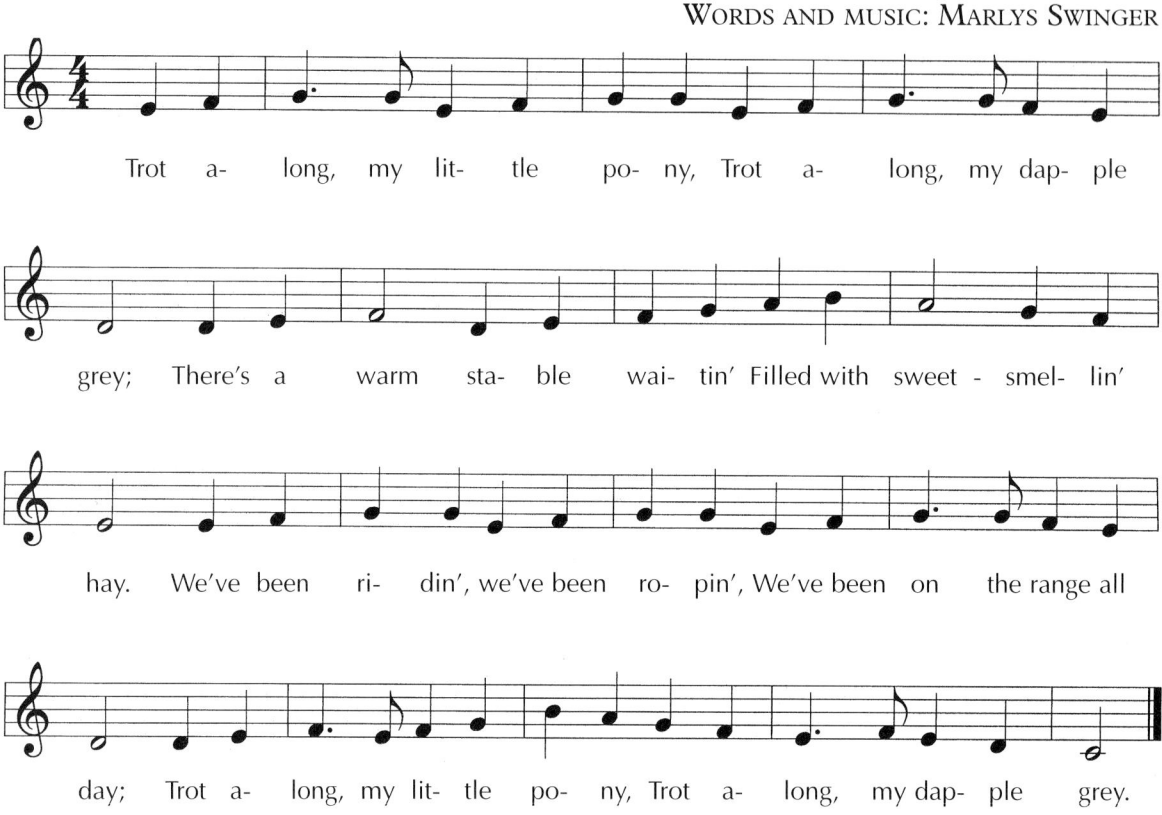

Trot a- long, my lit- tle po- ny, Trot a- long, my dap- ple

grey; There's a warm sta- ble wai- tin' Filled with sweet - smel- lin'

hay. We've been ri- din', we've been ro- pin', We've been on the range all

day; Trot a- long, my lit- tle po- ny, Trot a- long, my dap- ple grey.

Trot along, my little pony,
Trot along, my dapple grey;
There's a warm stable waitin'
Filled with sweet-smellin' hay.
We've been ridin', we've been ropin',
We've been on the range all day;
Trot along, my little pony,
Trot along, my dapple grey.

To get children to put their boots tidily in nursery, we chant:

'Noses by the wall and coats on the peg!'

Grand old Duke of York

CD TRACK 14

Oh the grand old Duke of York He had ten thou- sand men, He

marched them up to the top of the hill And he marched them down a- gain. And

when they were up, they were up And when they were down, they were down, And

when they were on- ly half way up, They were nei- ther up nor down.

Oh the grand old Duke of York
He had ten thousand men,
He marched them up to the top of the hill
And he marched them down again.
And when they were up, they were up
And when they were down, they were down,
And when they were only half way up
They were neither up nor down.

The policeman walks with heavy tread,
Left, right, left, right,
Swings his arms, holds up his head,
Left, right, left, right.

E. H. ADAMS

Skip to my lou

Skip, skip, skip to my lou
Skip, skip, skip to my lou
Skip, skip, skip to my lou
Skip to my lou, my darling.

(to the tune of *Skip to my Lou*)

A tall thin man, walking along,
Walking along, walking along.
A tall thin man, walking along,
Walking along the road.

A fat little frog jumping along,
Jumping along, jumping along,
A fat little frog jumping along,
Jumping along the road.

C. DAVIES

Make up more verses of your own.

Food and mealtimes

Carrots, potatoes, and cabbage and peas

CD TRACK 16

WORDS AND MUSIC: CANDY VERNEY

Carrots, po- tatoes, and cabbage and peas, Put in the soup, as much as you please;

Scrub them and clean them and chop them all fine, Boil in a saucepan with parsley and thyme.

Chopping vegetables

Carrots, potatoes, and cabbage and peas,
Put in the soup, as much as you please;
Scrub them and clean them and chop them
all fine,
Boil in a saucepan with parsley and thyme.

*I find calling the children to
meals by singing works far
better than any other way.*

Encouraging the child to eat

This is for Anna *(name of someone in your
family, including pets)*
This is for Dad
Off it goes, down the little red lane!

Little Robin Redbreast
Came to visit me;
This is what he whistled,
Thank you for my tea.

Davy Davy Dumpling,
Boil him in a pot,
Sugar him and butter him
And serve him very hot.

Mix a pancake,
Stir a pancake,
Pop it in the pan;
Fry a pancake,
Toss a pancake,
Catch it if you can!
CHRISTINA ROSSETTI

Three little puffins

CD TRACK 17

WORDS: ELEANOR FARJEON

MUSIC: MARLYS SWINGER

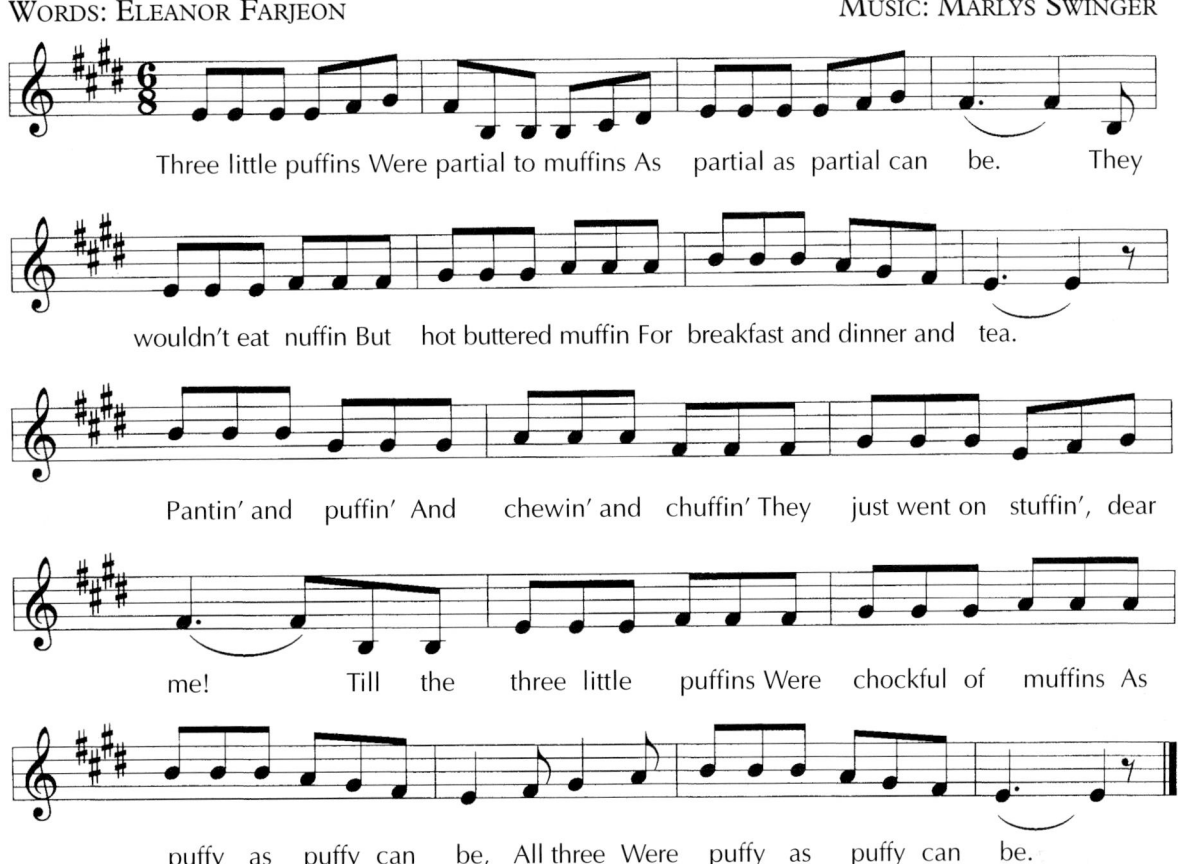

Three little puffins Were partial to muffins As partial as partial can be. They wouldn't eat nuffin But hot buttered muffin For breakfast and dinner and tea. Pantin' and puffin' And chewin' and chuffin' They just went on stuffin', dear me! Till the three little puffins Were chockful of muffins As puffy as puffy can be, All three Were puffy as puffy can be.

Three little puffins
Were partial to muffins
As partial as partial can be.
They wouldn't eat nuffin
But hot buttered muffin
For breakfast and dinner and tea.
Pantin' and puffin'
And chewin' and chuffin'
They just went on stuffin', dear me!
Till the three little puffins
Were chockful of muffins
As puffy as puffy can be,
All three
Were puffy as puffy can be.

Coo coo pigeons
Would you like some peas?
Here you are and there you are
As many as you please.
Coo coo pigeons
Was your dinner good?
Here you go and there you go
Off into the wood!

(from Japan)

Baking songs

Lovely yeast go to bed

CD TRACK 18

Lovely yeast, go to bed,
Wake again with a frothy head.

We roll it, we roll it

CD TRACK 19

We roll it, we roll it, we roll it very hard,
We bump it, we bump it, we bump it very hard,

We squeeze it, we squash it, we squeeze it very hard
We squeeze it, we squash it, we squeeze it very hard

It's ready, it's ready. It's ready to make into shapes.
It's ready, it's ready. It's ready to make into shapes.

Blow, wind, blow

MUSIC: CANDY VERNEY

Blow, wind, blow, and go, mill, go,
That the miller may grind his corn;
That the baker may take it,
And into bread bake it,
And bring us a loaf in the morn,
And bring us a loaf in the morn.

It's time to put our aprons on

To the tune of *Mulberry Bush* (see page 102)

It's time to put our aprons on,
Wash our hands, and aprons on.
It's time to put our aprons on
Ready to make the bread now.

Graces

TV, fast food and the haste of our busy lives easily erode family mealtimes, but maintaining these will give children the benefit of a daily pulse to their lives.

A moment's quiet before a meal builds family togetherness, fosters a sense of gratitude for our food, and encourages awareness of where it has come from.

For the golden corn

CD TRACK 22

WORDS: E. GOULD

MUSIC: E. SMITH

For the gol- den corn and the apples on the tree, For the

yel- low butter and the honey for our tea For fruits and nuts and ber-ries that

grow along the way, For birds and beasts and flow-ers, we thank you every day.

For the golden corn and the apples on the tree,
For the yellow butter and the honey for our tea
For fruits and nuts and berries that grow along the way,
For birds and beasts and flowers, we thank you every day.

Singing a grace settles the kids, joins us all together, and calms, ready to eat. The kids love it – it feels very special.

Blessings on the blossom

CD TRACK 23

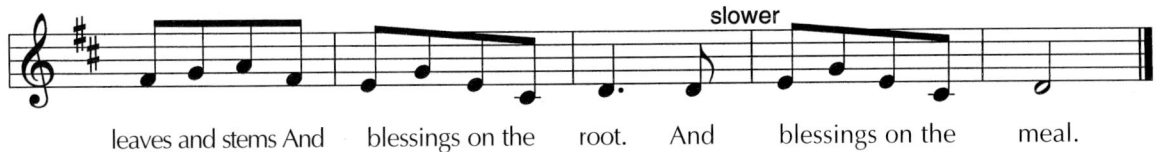

Blessings on the blossom
Blessings on the fruit,
Blessings on the leaves and stems
And blessings on the root.
And blessings on the meal.

Earth who gives to us our food

CD TRACK 24

MUSIC: CANDY VERNEY

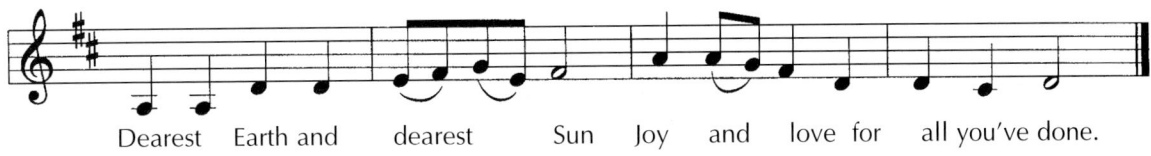

Earth who gives to us our food
Sun who makes it ripe and good
Dearest Earth and dearest Sun
Joy and love for all you've done.

Can be sung as a round; see note on page xxi.

Praise be God for Mother Earth

CD TRACK 25

WORDS: LAURENCE EDWARDS   MUSIC: CANDY VERNEY

Praise be God for Mother Earth, Who keeps us safe and well. Whose

mother heart all warm with love, Dark in her depths doth dwell.

Praise be God for Mother Earth,
Who keeps us safe and well.
Whose mother heart all warm with love,
Dark in her depths doth dwell.

For health and strength and daily food

CD TRACK 26

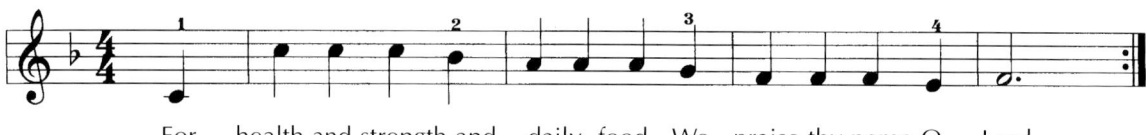

For   health and strength and   daily food   We   praise thy name O   Lord.

For health and strength and daily food
We praise thy name O Lord.

Can be sung as a round; see note on page xxi.

For sun and rain
For grass and grain
For all who toil
On sea and soil
That we may eat this daily food
We give our loving thanks to God.

Johnny Appleseed

CD TRACK 27

Oh the Lord is good to me
And so I thank the Lord
For giving me
The things I need
The rain, the sun
And the apple seed
The Lord is good to me.

*Based on the American legend of Johnny
Appleseed, who is said to have walked barefoot
from coast to coast carrying his Bible and a sack
of apple seeds, which he planted as he travelled.*

Are we ready

CD TRACK 28

To the tune of *Frère Jacques*

Are we rea-dy, are we rea-dy, Holding hands to-gether, holding hands to-gether,

Ready to light the candle, ready to light the candle Bless our meal, bless our meal.

Are we ready, are we ready,
Holding hands together, holding hands together,
Ready to light the candle, ready to light the candle
Bless our meal, bless our meal.

The very little ones like lighting a candle and
finger rhymes before a meal, as it helps them to
be quiet. For example: 'Two little dicky birds',
'Up the tall white candlestick', etc.

Other household activities

We fostered several children. I always knew when they had settled in, because they would start to sing. It signified to me that they were relaxed and happy.

Higgledy Piggledy Pop

CD TRACK 29

To the tune of *Hickory Dickory Dock*

Higgledy piggledy pop! The dog has swallowed the mop! The
pig's in a hurry The cat's in a flurry, Higgledy piggledy pop!

Higgledy piggledy pop!
The dog has swallowed the mop!
The pig's in a hurry
The cat's in a flurry,
Higgledy piggledy pop!

I used to get hiccups a lot as a child and my Dad used to make up words to well known tunes and we would sing – my memory is that this was often when washing up. Anyway, my children all got hiccups a lot and they used to try and sing something like 'Baa Baa Black Sheep' as far as they could without hiccupping; and this either stopped them or caused such giggles when hiccups interrupted the song, it was good fun.

Can you tell me

CD TRACK 30

Can you tell me, can you tell me What the mum- mies are
La la la...

do- ing? They are sweeping, they are sweeping And we can sweep too!

Can you tell me, can you tell me
What the mummies are doing?
They are sweeping, they are sweeping
And we can sweep too!
La la la...

Can you tell me, can you tell me
What the daddies are doing?
They are cleaning, they are cleaning,
And we can clean too!
La la la...

To the tune of *Mulberry Bush* (see page 102,
CD TRACK 87)

This is the way we wash our hands etc
This is the way we tidy our toys etc

Can you tell me, can you tell me
What the grannies are doing?
They are cooking, they are cooking
And we can cook too!
La la la...

With my little broom I sweep, sweep, sweep,
With my little toes I creep, creep, creep,
With my little eyes I peep, peep, peep,
The bedroom clean we'll keep, keep, keep.

We gnomes are working happily

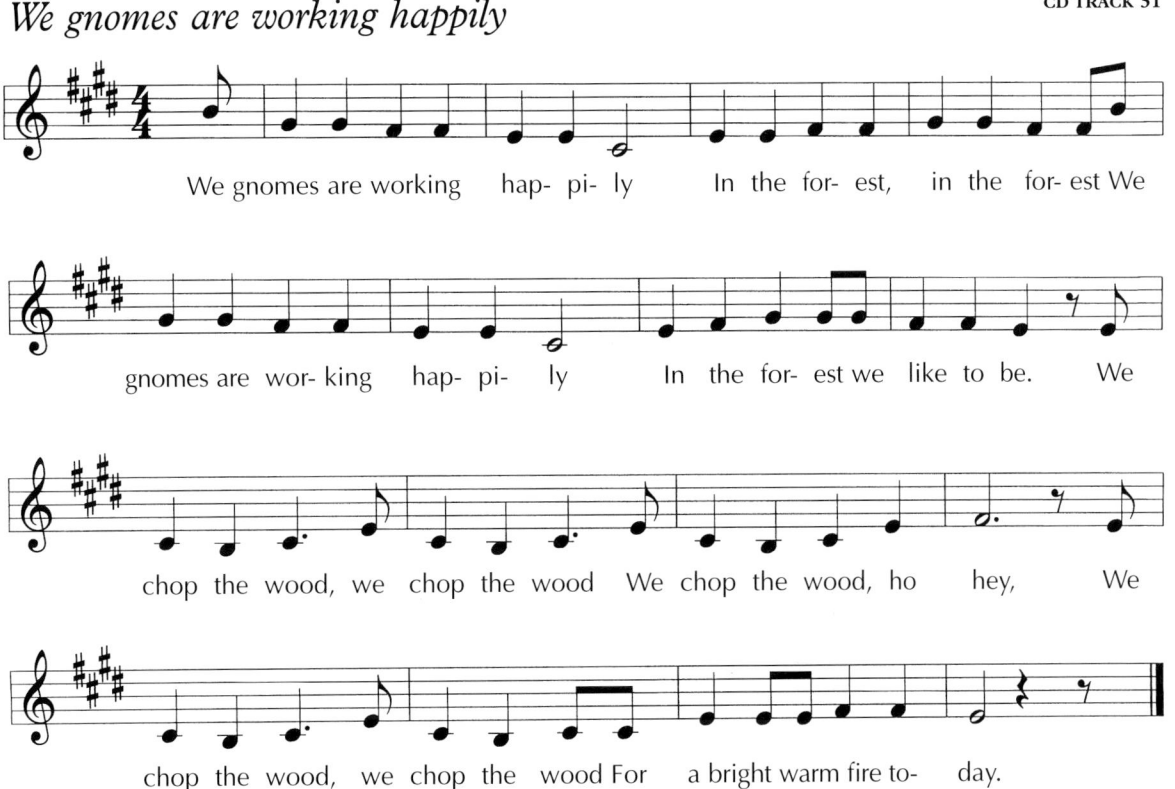

We gnomes are working happily
In the forest, in the forest
We gnomes are working happily
In the forest we like to be.
We chop the wood, we chop the wood
We chop the wood, ho hey,
We chop the wood, we chop the wood
For a bright warm fire today.

We gnomes are working happily
In our cottage, in our cottage
We gnomes are working happily
In our cottage we like to be.
We sweep the floor, we sweep the floor
We sweep the floor ho hey,
We sweep the floor, we sweep the floor
Spotlessly clean today.

We gnomes are working happily
In our kitchen, in our kitchen,
We gnomes are working happily
In our kitchen we like to be.
We stir the pot, we stir the pot,
We stir the pot today,
We stir the pot, we stir the pot,
For the best meal of the day.

Freely adapt to suit the task in hand.

Dashing away with a smoothing iron

TRADITIONAL ENGLISH

'Twas on a Mon- day morn- ing When I beheld my dar- ling, She

looked so neat and charm- ing In ev- ery high deg- ree; She looked so neat and

nim- ble, O Wash-ing out her lin- en, O Dashing a- way with the smooth- ing iron

Dashing a- way with the smooth-ing iron She stole my heart a- way.

1. 'Twas on a Monday morning
   When I beheld my darling,
   She looked so neat and charming
   In every high degree;
   She looked so neat and nimble, O
   Washing out her linen, O

CHORUS
   Dashing away with the smoothing iron
   Dashing away with the smoothing iron
   She stole my heart away.

2. 'Twas on a Tuesday morning
   When I beheld my darling,
   She looked so neat and charming
   In every high degree;
   She looked so neat and nimble, O
   Hanging out her linen, O

3. 'Twas on a Wednesday morning…
   Starching of her linen, O

4. 'Twas on a Thursday morning…
   Ironing of her linen, O

5. 'Twas on a Friday morning…
   Folding of her linen, O

6. 'Twas on a Saturday morning
   Airing of her linen, O

7. 'Twas on a Sunday morning
   Wearing of her linen, O

Busy pixies

WORDS AND MUSIC: S. DAVIES

Now's the time to ti- dy up. Let's be bus- y pix- ies,

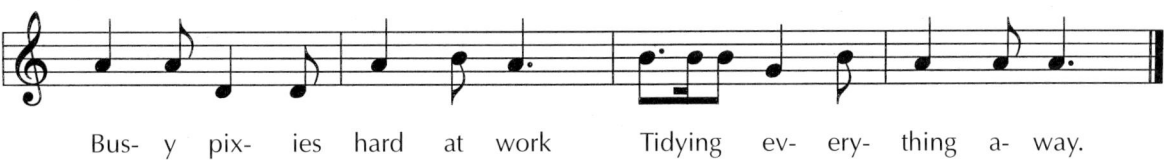

Bus- y pix- ies hard at work Tidying ev- ery- thing a- way.

Now's the time to tidy up.
Let's be busy pixies,
Busy pixies hard at work
Tidying everything away.

As you fold the cloth:

Butterfly, butterfly fold your wings

As you shake out the cloth:

1 2 3 big butterfly!

Wash the dishes, wipe the dishes,
Ring the bell for tea;
Three good wishes, three good kisses,
I will give to thee.

Daytime sleep

Sleep my little one, sleep

CD TRACK **34**

Sleep my little one, sleep
Under the bright blue sky,
Mother Earth shall watch over you,
Harm shall ne'er come by.

Car journeys

Several people have said: 'Long songs for car journeys'. Here are some suggestions:

- What shall we do with the drunken sailor?
- The Rattling Bog.
- Green grow the rushes oh!
- I had a cat and the cat pleased me
- When I first came to this land
- We all live in a yellow submarine
- The wheels on the bus
- Doh, a Deer

We started singing to Michael in the car when he was 4 months old and we were driving up to the North West Highlands. Anything with actions goes down a treat, especially if the actions involve him. His absolute favourite game is for us to sing one of his well-known songs really badly, stuttering over the words, drawling the notes or just stopping as if we don't know what's coming next, then coming in very suddenly. This has him in fits and pointing eagerly for more.

Our whole family made up rhyming songs. Someone would start with a line, e.g.

The little old lady was very fat.

Then someone else would add:

When she was knitting she always sat,

And another might say

And wore a silly, silly hat.

The songs were very silly, but we all enjoyed them immensely and it passed the time.

Did you ever see a lassie

CD TRACK 35

TRADITIONAL

Did you e- ver see a las- sie, a las- sie, a

las- sie, Did you e- ver see a las- sie go this way and

that. Go this way and that way, Go this way and that way, Did you

e- ver see a las- sie go this way and that?

Did you ever see a lassie, a lassie, a lassie,
Did you ever see a lassie go this way and that.
Go this way and that way,
Go this way and that way,
Did you ever see a lassie go this way and that?

Did you ever see a laddie, a laddie, a laddie...

Did you ever see a funny man...

Did you ever see a soldier...

Did you ever see a clown... etc

*Each person in the car takes it in turns to do an
action, all the others copy it.*

*On long car journeys when I was
young, my Mum would sing 'The
Gypsy Rover'. As we got older, it
became a light-hearted threat: 'If
you don't hurry up, I'll start singing
the Gypsy Rover!'*

There's a fox in a box

CD TRACK 36

There's a fox in a box in my little bed My little bed, my little bed There's a

fox in a box in my little bed And there isn't much room for me.

It changes the mood from boredom to happiness on a long car journey if we make up songs. The first verse will be a real song e.g.

There's a fox in a box in my little bed
My little bed, my little bed
There's a fox in a box in my little bed
And there isn't much room for me.

Then we rack our brains for other animals and things to rhyme with them e.g. A frog on a log.

On long drives down from Vancouver Island to California, to see Grandma, we used to sing the kids' names in rhythm. Also make up songs that helped the kids have a measure of how far we had got e.g.

Are we almost at Campbell River
Are we almost at Campbell River
Are we almost at Campbell River
Where we cross the bridge?

Yes we're almost there at Campbell River... etc.

Faces

When she was very young I'd hum a deep sound against Annie's body – you know how the sound vibrates right through you. When she was about two I'd start with a hum, and she would copy it. If I changed pitch, she'd follow,

and so on. As she got older, she'd take the lead sometimes and the patterns got more complex, and we'd overlap the sounds. Great fun and completely spontaneous.

Here sits the Lord Mayor, *(nose)*
Here sit his men *(eyes)*
Here sits the cock *(ears)*
And here sits the hen.
Here sit the little chicks *(teeth)*
Here they run in, *(mouth)*
Chin-chopper, chin-chopper *(chin)*
Chin-chopper chin.

Tae titly,
Little fitty,
Shin sharpy,
Knee knapy,
Hinchie pinchie,
Wymie bulgy,
Breast berry,
Chin cherry,
Moo merry,
Nose nappy,
Ee winky,
Broo brinky,
Ower the croon,
And awa' wi' it.

Knock at the door, *(forehead)*
Peep in, *(eyes)*
Lift the latch, *(nose)*
Walk in. *(mouth)*

Knees, feet and toes

Why infants should like having the soles of
their feet patted they alone know...

Shoe a little horse

CD TRACK 37

NURSERY RHYME   MUSIC: CANDY VERNEY

Shoe a little horse,   Shoe a little mare,   But   let the little colt go   bare, bare, bare.

Shoe a little horse,
Shoe a little mare,
But let the little colt go bare, bare, bare.

Tickly, tickly, on your knee,
If you laugh you don't love me.

Hob, shoe, hob;
Hob, shoe, hob;
Here a nail, there a nail,
And that's well shod.

If you are a gentleman,
As I suppose you be,
You'll neither laugh nor smile
At the tickling of your knee.

I can hear my feet go tap, tap, tap,
I can hear my knees go slap, slap, slap,
I can hear my hands go clap, clap, clap,
But I can't hear my head go nod, nod, nod.

*The simplest of rhymes, but children are
entranced by the silence of the last line.*

Cobbler, cobbler

CD TRACK 38

NURSERY RHYME

MUSIC: CANDY VERNEY

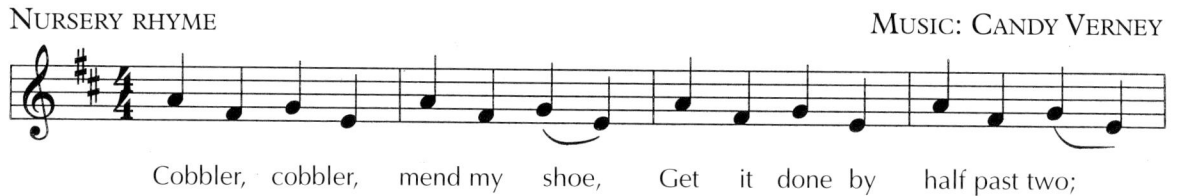

Cobbler, cobbler, mend my shoe, Get it done by half past two;

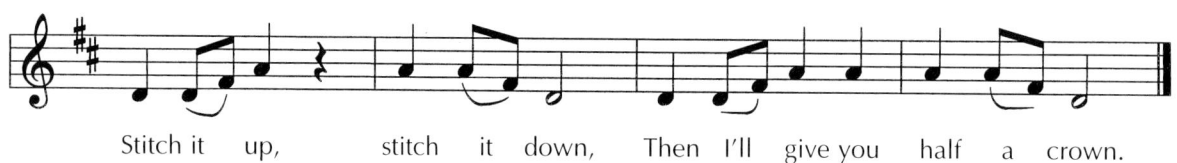

Stitch it up, stitch it down, Then I'll give you half a crown.

Cobbler, cobbler, mend my shoe,
Get it done by half past two;
Stitch it up, stitch it down,
Then I'll give you half a crown.

See-saw, Margery Daw,
The old hen flew over the malthouse;
She counted her chickens one by one,
Still she missed the little white one,
And this is it, this is it, this is it.

See-saw, sacradown,
Which is the way to London town?
One foot up and the other foot down,
That is the way to London town.

Tit-tat-toe,
My first go,
Three jolly butcher boys
All in a row;
Stick one up,
Stick one down,
Stick one in the old man's crown.

This little pig had a rub-a-dub,
This little pig had a scrub-a-scrub,
This little pig-a-wig ran upstairs,
This little pig-a-wig called out, Bears!
Down came the jar with loud Slam! Slam!
And this little pig had all the jam.

Finger games

Finger games develop coordination and dexterity and are also a first step towards acting out stories and songs, using something very close to hand! They calm and focus children, creating an immediate absorption in their own activity.

5 fingers

Tom Thumbkin
Willie Wilkin
Long Daniel
Betty Bodkin
And Little Dick.

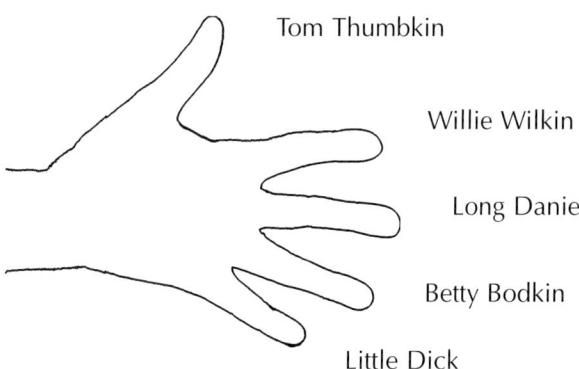

Tom Thumbkin

Willie Wilkin

Long Daniel

Betty Bodkin

Little Dick

Round about, and round about, here sits the hare, *(circle finger around baby's*
In the corner of a cornfield and that's just there.   *palm close to thumb)*
This little dog found her, *(fingers, starting with the thumb)*
This little dog ran after her,
This little dog caught her,
This little dog ate her,
And this little dog said,
Give me a little bit please. *(run up baby's arm)*

Mrs Mouse was cooking rice (*circle finger around baby's palm*)
For her little babies
She gave some to this little one (*point to each finger*)
She gave some to this little one
She gave some to this little one
She gave some to this little one
But when she came to this little one
She ran to the shop to get some more. (*run up baby's arm*)

Once I saw a little bird
Come hop, hop, hop,
And I cried, Little bird
Will you stop, stop, stop?

I was going to the window
To say, How do you do?
But he shook his little tail
And away he flew.

My father was a Frenchman (*hold child's hand, and swing*)
A Frenchman, a Frenchman,
My father was a Frenchman,
And he bought me a fiddle. (*hold child's arm straight*)
He cut it here (*cut above and below elbow*)
He cut it there
He cut it through the middle. (*bend child's arm up*)

Let's build a house...   *(shape house with arms)*

We dig the ground,
   diggety dig, diggety dig,   *(imitate digging)*

We start to build, brick by brick,   *(clenched fists, one
   brick by brick,   on top of another)*

We hang the door, eeeh, eeeh,   *(swing arms side to side)*
   (*or* squeak, squeak,)

We put on the roof,
   bangety bang, bangety bang,   *(clap hands)*

And a chimney on top...   *(one arm straight up)*

That's it *(hands out)*
We stop! *(arms crossed)*

Our house is finished for all to see.   *(arms open wide)*

Let's go inside and have a cup of tea.   *(imitate sipping tea)*

*This can also be done with larger movements standing in a
circle. For last 2 lines, all go into middle and sit down.*

CANDY VERNEY

Apple pie, apple pie,
Mary likes apple pie;
So do I, so do I. (*2 fingers creep up the arm, over the head, to the chin*)

Put your finger in foxy's hole, (*interweave fingers, leaving a little 'hole'*)
Foxy's not at home;
Foxy's at the back door
Picking a marrow bone.
If the child puts her finger in the hole, she gets a little nip from the thumbnail below.

This is the boat, the golden boat (*hands cupped, rocking*)
That sailed the sea, the silvery sea. (*hands up and down*)
Here are the oars of ivory white (*fingers interlocked, upwards*)
That lift and dip, that lift and dip (*hands up and down*)
Here are the ten little fairy men (*fingers*)
Running along, running along, (*run fingers forward*)
That take the oars of ivory white
That lift and dip, that lift and dip,
That take the boat, the golden boat
Over the silvery sea.

Can be sung to tune of *I had a little nut tree*

I had a little cherry stone
And put it in the ground.

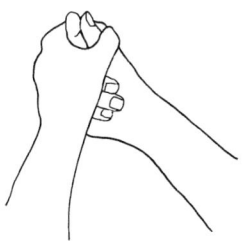

Next time I came to look at it
A tiny shoot I found.

The shoot grew upwards day by day,
Until it was a tree.
I picked the rosy cherries off
And had them for my tea. Yum yum!

Five little eggs in a nest of straw
One egg hatched and then there were four.

Four little eggs in a nest in a tree
One egg hatched and then there were three.

Three little eggs all speckled blue
One egg hatched and then there were two.

Two little eggs from where little chicks come
One egg hatched and then there was one.

One little egg lying in the sun
That egg hatched and then there were none.

Roly poly ever so slowly (*roll hands round each other*)
Ever so slowly,
Roly poly up up up
Roly poly down down down.
Roly poly up to my nosey, up to my nosey,
Roly poly down to my toesy, down to my toesy,
Roly poly into my tummy, into my tummy.
Roly poly faster and faster and faster and faster (*gradually get faster, pausing before...*)
And stop!   *bringing hands down onto lap)*

Open shut them

O- pen shut them   O- pen shut them   Give a lit- tle

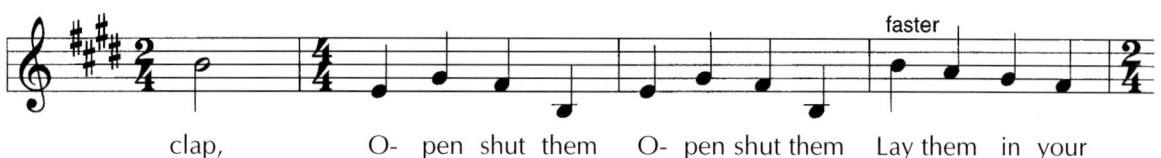

clap,   O- pen shut them   O- pen shut them   Lay them in your

lap.   Creep them, creep them Creep them, creep them Right up to your

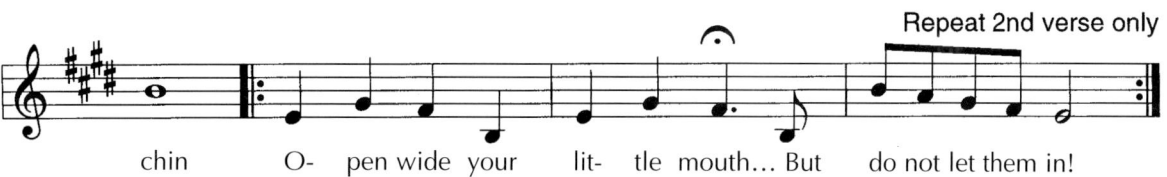

chin   O- pen wide your   lit- tle mouth... But   do not let them in!

Open shut them
Open shut them
Give a little clap,
Open shut them
Open shut them
Lay them in your lap.
Creep them, creep them *(faster)*
Creep them, creep them
Right up to your chin
Open wide your little mouth... *(pause)*
But do not let them in! *(fast)*

Shut them, open,
Shut them, open
Up to shoulders fly,
Let them like a sparrow flutter
Flutter in the sky.
Falling, falling, falling, falling
Nearly to the ground
Slowly pick them up again
And turn them round and round and
Slowly turn them round and round
                    (getting very slow)
Faster, faster, faster. *(roll as quickly as possible)*

5 little mice

CD TRACK 40

WORDS: EMILLE POULSSON   MUSIC: CANDY VERNEY

Five little mice on the kitchen floor, Seeking breadcrumbs or something more;

Five little mice on the shelf up high, Feasting so daintily on a pie – But the

slow down

big round eyes of the wise old cat See what the five little mice are at.

faster   *slow down*

Quickly she jumps! – but the mice run away, And hide in their snug little holes all day.

Five little mice on the kitchen floor,

Seeking breadcrumbs or something more;

48

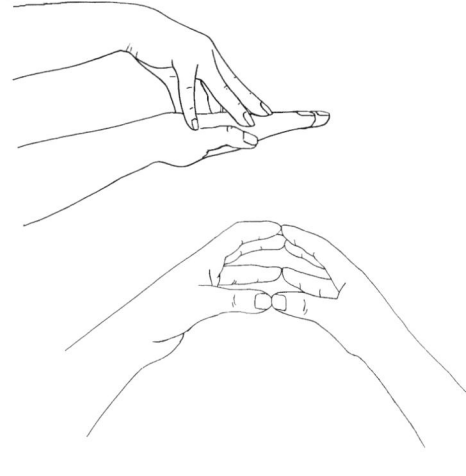

Five little mice on the shelf up high,

Feasting so daintily on a pie –

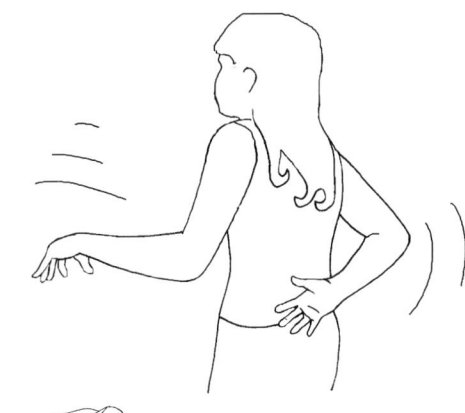

But the big round eyes of the wise old cat

See what the five little mice are at.

Quickly she jumps! – but the mice run away,

And hide in their snug little holes all day.

Here is the church, and there is the steeple; *(fingers interlocked inwards,*
forefingers pointing up)

Open the door and here are the people. *(open thumbs, and reverse hands,*
so that fingers are upwards)

Here is the parson going upstairs, *(place hands back to back, intertwine*
fingers one by one)

And here he is saying his prayers. *(twist hands round, so that they are*
knotted, and thumb is the parson
in the pulpit, from where he gives
a sermon on potato peeling:)

'Dearly beloved brethren, is it not a sin, *(wiggle thumb to*
When you peel potatoes to throw away the skin? *show parson giving*
For the skin feeds the pigs, and pigs feed you. *a sermon)*
Dearly beloved brethren, is this not true?'

Here are the lady's knives and forks, *(fingers interlaced, facing upwards)*
Here is the lady's table, *(turn hands over)*
Here is the lady's looking-glass, *(lift up baby fingers, to make arch)*
And here is the baby's cradle. *(raise forefingers as well, and rock)*

Dandling and other games

One of the games that most thrilled me was when my father would give me a 'Round the World'. It involved my standing with my legs wide apart, bending down and putting my arms through my legs. My father would stand behind me, get hold of my hands and pull my arms upwards, causing me to flip 360 degrees, hence round the world.
(Not advisable for very young children, and be careful of their heads.)

Sit child on your knees, facing you, and hold her hands.

This is the way the ladies ride
Nim, nim, nim.
This is the way the gentlemen ride,
Trim, trim, trim;
This is the way the farmers ride
Hobble-de-hoy, hobble-de-hoy
This is the way the ploughboys ride
Hobbledy, hobbledy, hobbledy;
This is the way the highwayman rides
Gallop, a-gallop, a-gallop;
This is the way *Charlie* rides,
Gallop, a-gallop, a-whooeee!

Sometimes you can add:
They come to a hedge, and wheee they jump over!
They come to a muddy place and slippery-slide, slippery-slide!

Little girls go nim, nim, nim,
Little boys go trot, trot, trot,
Ladies go cantery, cantery, cantery... *(as long as you like)*
Gentlemen go gallopy, gallopy, gallopy... *(louder and louder, and crash)*

Dance to your daddy

TRADITIONAL

Dance to your daddy My little babby Dance to your daddy

My little lamb. You shall have a fishy In a little dishy
You shall have an apple You shall have a plum

You shall have a fishy When the boat comes in.
You shall have a basket When your daddy comes home.

Dance to your daddy
My little babby
Dance to your daddy
My little lamb.

You shall have a fishy
In a little dishy
You shall have a fishy
When the boat comes in.

You shall have an apple
You shall have a plum
You shall have a basket
When your daddy comes home.

Laugh my baby beauty,
What will time do to ye?
Furrow your cheek
Wrinkle your neck,
So laugh my baby beauty.

To market, to market
To buy a fat pig,
Home again, home again
Jiggety-jig.
To market, to market
To buy a fat hog,
Home again, home again,
Jiggety-jog.

I've been to Harlem

TRADITIONAL

I've been to Har- lem,   I've been to Do- ver,   I've travelled this wide world all   o-   ver

O- ver,   o-   ver,   this world o- ver, Drink what you have to drink And turn your glasses o- ver.

I've been to Harlem,   (*sit cross-legged, and child rides on your foot*)
I've been to Dover,
I've travelled this wide world all over
Over, over, this world over,
Drink what you have to drink
And turn your glasses over. (*toss child in air, and swap feet*)

A trot, and a canter, a gallop, and over,
Out of the saddle, and roll in the clover.

Mama and Papa and Uncle John
Went to market, one by one.
Mama fell off, (*one side*
Papa fell off (*other side*)
And Uncle John went gallopy, gallopy, gallopy.... (*on and on*)

Back ride, adult is the donkey!

To the tune of *Horsey, horsey* (see page 13, CD TRACK 12)

Donkey, donkey, do not bray,
Mend your pace and trot away,
Indeed, the market's almost done,
My butter's melting in the sun. *(collapse, or tip child off)*

A farmer went trotting upon his gray mare,
Bumpety, bumpety, bump!
With his daughter behind him so rosy and fair,
Lumpety, lumpety, lump!

A raven cried, Croak! And they all tumbled down,
Bumpety, bumpety, bump!
The mare broke her knees and the farmer his crown,
Lumpety, lumpety, lump!

The mischievous raven flew laughing away,
Bumpety, bumpety, bump!
And vowed he would serve them the same the next day,
Lumpety, lumpety, lump!

Dickery, dickery dare

CD TRACK 43

To the tune of *Hickory Dickory Dock* (see page 27)

Dickery, dickery, dare,
The pig flew up in the air;
The man in brown soon brought him down,
Dickery, dickery, dare.

Rig a jig jig

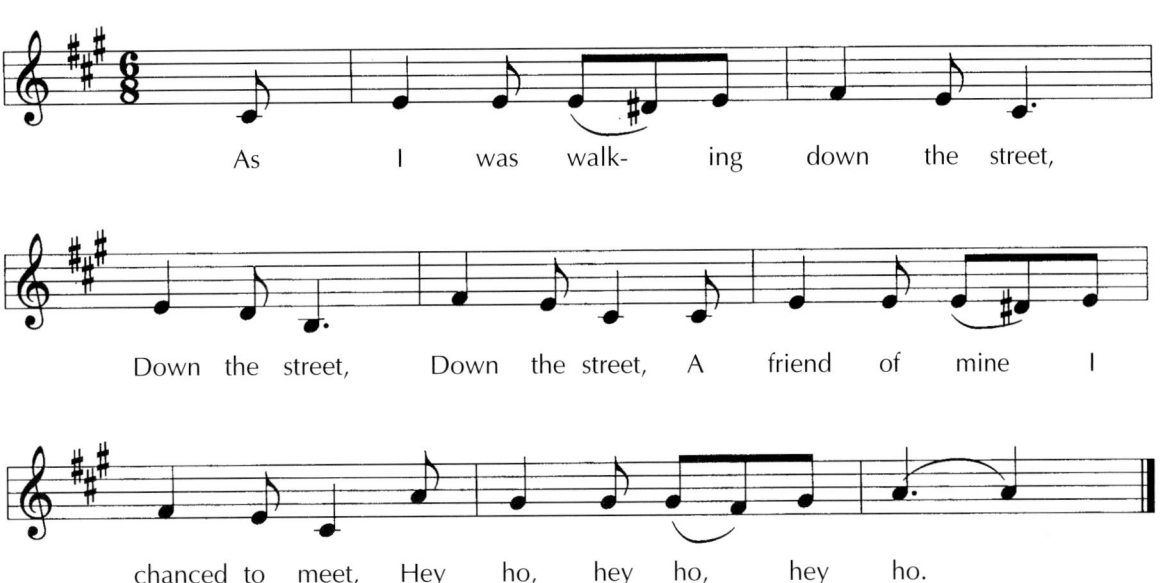

As I was walking down the street, *(gentle bouncing)*
Down the street,
Down the street,
A friend of mine I chanced to meet,
Hey ho, hey ho, hey ho.

Rig a jig jig and away we go, *(higher, higher!)*
Away we go
Away we go
Rig a jig jig and away we go,
Hey ho, hey ho, hey ho.

Ride a cock-horse
To Banbury Cross,
To see what Tommy can buy;
A penny white loaf,
A penny white cake,
And a twopenny apple-pie.

Tinga layo!

TRADITIONAL CARIBBEAN

Tin-ga lay- o! Come, lit- tle don-key, come. Tin- ga

lay- o! Come, little donkey, come. Me donkey buck, Me donkey

Fine

leap, Me donkey kick wid him two hind feet. Me donkey

D.C. al Fine

buck, Me donkey leap, Me donkey kick wid him two hind feet.

Foot or back ride

Tinga layo! Come, little donkey, come.
Tinga layo! Come, little donkey, come.
Me donkey buck,
Me donkey leap,
Me donkey kick wid him two hind feet.
Me donkey buck,
Me donkey leap,
Me donkey kick wid him two hind feet.
Tinga layo! Come, little donkey, come.
Tinga layo! Come, little donkey, come.

American jump, American jump,
One- two- three.
Under the water, under the sea,
Catching fishes for my tea:
Dead,
Or, Alive,
Or, Round the World?

The child holds the grownup's hands and is jumped up and down. On 'three', she has an extra big jump and twists her legs around the adult's waist. Let the child's body fall backwards.

She is asked, 'Dead or alive or round the world.'
If she chooses 'Dead', she is (carefully) dropped onto the floor.
For 'Alive', pull her upright.
For 'Round the world', whirl her round as long as possible.

When they were babies, humming often settled them from crying more quickly than singing. Perhaps they felt the vibration of my hum as I held them.

German dandling song:

Hoppe hoppe Reiter,
Wenn er fällt, dann schreit er!
Fällt er in den Graben,
Fressen ihn die Raben,
Fällt er in den Sumpf,
Macht der Reiter plumps!

Translation:
Jump, jump, rider!
When he falls he shouts;
If he falls into the ditch,
The ravens eat him up;
If he falls into the swamp,
The rider goes bump.

Evening

I was brought up after the war on a farm in Germany managed by my mother and her sister. I have a vivid memory, aged six or seven, of sitting on the cart, after work was done in the evening, and being pulled slowly homeward by two cows. The track followed the contour of a hill, and then suddenly there was the village stretched out below us in the valley, with hills way beyond. The sun had already gone down, and the sky was filled with colours that gave signs of the coming night. As the twitter of birds died down, the only sounds left were the creaking of the cart, the crickets in the grass and the slow plodding of the cows' hoofs. Then my mother would sing this song (see next page), 'Es ist so still geworden'. Life is much noisier now, but whenever I sing it, the silence I experienced as a child comes back to me.

Which is the way to fairyland?

CD TRACK 46

Which is the way to fai- ry- land, To fai- ry- land, to fai- ry- land,

Which is the way to fai- ry- land To dance by the light of the moon?

Which is the way to fairyland,
To fairyland, to fairyland,
Which is the way to fairyland
To dance by the light of the moon?

Up the hill and down the lane
Down the lane, down the lane,
Up the hill and down the lane
You'll get there very soon.

Over the stile into the wood... etc
You'll get there very soon.

Here we are in fairyland... etc
We'll dance by the light of the moon

Sing some of the verses before telling a story

Es ist so still geworden

TRADITIONAL GERMAN

Es ist so still ge- wor- den, ver- rauscht das Abend- wehn. Da

hört man al- ler- or- ten der En- gel Füsse geh- en. Rings

in die Ta- le senkt sich die Fin- ster- nis mit Macht. Wirf

ab, mein Herz, was dich krän- ket, Wirf ab, mein Herz, was dir bange macht.

Es ist so still geworden, verrauscht das Abendwehn.
Da hört man allerorten der Engel Füsse gehen.
Rings in die Tale senkt sich die Finsternis mit Macht.
Wirf ab, mein Herz, was dich kränket,
Wirf ab, mein Herz, was dir bange macht.

Translation:
The evening has become so still,
One hears angels everywhere.
Dusk wraps its gentle cloak about the valley.
My heart: cast off all harm
My heart: cast off all fear.

In the evening

CD TRACK 47

WORDS: IVY O. EASTWICK   MUSIC: CANDY VERNEY

In the evening The sun goes down, And the lamps are lit A- round the town. The

bats fly low Round the grey church dome, The thrush and the black- bird Are safe- ly home. Are

safe- ly home In their qui- et nest – The thrush and the black-bird Are both at rest.

In the evening
The sun goes down,
And the lamps are lit
Around the town.

The bats fly low
Round the grey church dome,
The thrush and the blackbird
Are safely home.

Are safely home
In their quiet nest –
The thrush and the blackbird
Are both at rest.

Getting undressed

This is a game that never fails to delight little
ones, from two years old right up to eight or
so (see Introduction).

Oh! A-hunting we will go

Oh!   A-   hun- ting we will   go,   A- cross the fields of   snow,   We'll

catch a   fox and   put him in a box And   then we'll let   him   go!

Oh! A-hunting we will go,
Across the fields of snow,
We'll catch a fox and put him in a box
And then we'll let him go!

*Adult sits on a chair near a bed or wall, so that
a passage is made. Swing arm slowly in the gap,
in time with the song. Child runs through the
gap, trying not to be caught.*

This can be used as a great way to undress
reluctant children – if you catch them, you
are allowed to take off one bit of their
clothing!

I wiggle my fingers
I wiggle my toes,
I wiggle my shoulders,
I wiggle my nose.
Now all the wiggles are gone from me
And I'm as still as I can be.

*I use this song when the kids are very
high, and need to calm down. It works
brilliantly.*

Diddle diddle dumpling, my son John,
Went to bed with his trousers on;
One shoe off and one shoe on,
Diddle diddle dumpling, my son John.

Bath time

A bath time game which I loved as a child was 'The Sack of Potatoes'. After getting out of the bath, I would sit in a large bath towel laid out on the bathroom floor. My father gathered up the four corners securely, and threw the towel and me over his shoulder, muttering: 'Oh this sack of potatoes is SO heavy...' and carried me off to bed. One day when I asked for it, my father replied, 'You're too heavy for that game now!' I can still remember the disappointment.

I met a little duck

CD TRACK **49**

WORDS AND MUSIC: ESTHER I. NELSON

I met a litt- le duck one day And he said, 'Quack, quack.'

I met a little duck one day
And he said, 'Quack, quack.'

I said, 'Will you come home with me?'
But he said, 'Quack, quack.'

I said, 'Do you swim around all day?'
And he said, 'Quack, quack.'

'Is Mister Fox a friend of yours?'
But he said, 'Quack, quack.'

I said, 'Do you have baby ducks?'
And he said, 'Quack, quack.'

This can be a game, where the child nods her head for yes, or shakes her head for no, on the quacks.

Rub a dub dub
Three babes in a tub
Who do you think got wet?
The daddy, the mummy,
The teddy bear's tummy,
Hoppity, out you get.

Chug, chug, chug,
I'm a little tug,
I pull the big boats,
Chug, chug, chug.

Rub-dub-dub, three men in a tub, (*rubbing dry with a towel*)
And who do you think they be?
The butcher, the baker, the candlestick maker,
Turn 'em out knaves all three!

Hair washing

Annie hated having her hair washed, but the singing really helped to distract her and make it fun. She also loved 'The big ship sailed on the ally ally oh'.

We used to sing 'I'm going to wash that man right out of my hair!' to accompany hair washing – a little sexist but it worked!

Teeth-cleaning songs

The songs we use for teeth-cleaning are: 'Daisy, Daisy, give me your answer do', and 'Row, row, row your boat'

We had a problem with a foster child of five who had never cleaned her teeth. She would clench her teeth together and refuse to open her mouth. I made up a song about teeth cleaning, special to her. From then on, once she heard the song, she laughed and gave in willingly. She felt it as a reward.

...and finger nails

When I cut the boys' fingernails, I used to say: 'This little pig went to market'

This is a game I play with Danny, my grandson aged two, to lure him into the bath. It's a way of getting him upstairs, because he doesn't like the thought of going to bed, and it's a sign that that's what is going to happen next. The rhyme seems important because it becomes a song, and he loves the repetition of it. It's a ritual we do, just the two of us, a bond between us:

Where's the green frog? Is it behind the door?
    No...
Is it on the floor?
    No...
Is it in the drawer?
    Yes!

Going to bed

Upstairs to fairyland

CD TRACK 50

Upstairs   to   fairyland,   Mind how   you   go.

Hold tight to Mummy's hand,   Walk on   tiptoe.   Get your tickets ready to

Pass   through   the   nursery gate,   Quiet   as   a   mouse.

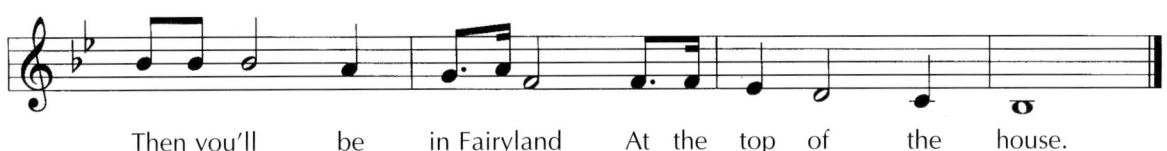

Then you'll   be   in Fairyland   At the top of   the   house.

Upstairs to fairyland,
Mind how you go.
Hold tight to Mummy's hand,
Walk on tiptoe.
Get your tickets ready to
Pass through the nursery gate,
Quiet as a mouse.
Then you'll be in Fairyland
At the top of the house.

This song was sung to my mother when she was little, and she was born in 1924 in Herefordshire. She sang it to me, and I sang it to my little boy, who is now seventeen and six foot three!

Up the wooden hill to Bedfordshire

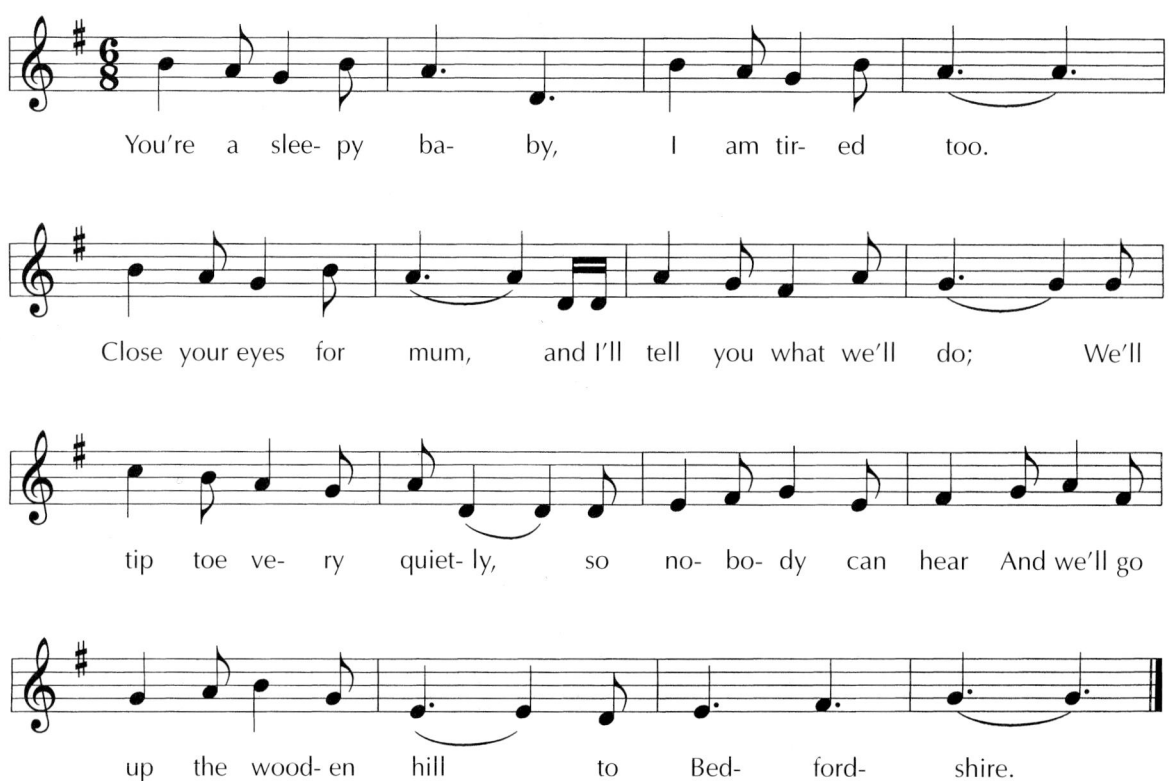

You're a sleepy baby, I am tired too.
Close your eyes for mum, and I'll tell you what we'll do;
We'll tiptoe very quietly, so nobody can hear
And we'll go up the wooden hill to Bedfordshire.

I see the moon

CD TRACK 52

I see the moon The moon sees me; God bless the moon, And God bless me.

I see the moon
The moon sees me;
God bless the moon,
And God bless me.

When I weaned Clare, I used to sing more, to recreate the safe, enclosed, gentle, relaxing feeling which would prepare her for sleep.

Tu-whitt, tu-whitt, tu-whoo tu-whoo,
Good night to me, good night to you.
'Tis the old white owl in the ivy tree,
But I can't see him, and he can't see me.
ERSKINE CRUM

If we were going for a walk in the dark or dusk, I used to sing to Jerome sometimes to reassure him, as he didn't like this time of day much when little. 'The Lord is my Shepherd' is very comforting.

Getting into bed rhyme:

Shadrach, Mishach, and Abedwigo! (*toss child into bed*)

Lullabies

I sang lullabies to my eldest son for half an hour to settle him to sleep, from birth to 2-3 years. He was a very light sleeper. Later on, he was a beautiful singer, and in the choir at secondary school. My third son was an even worse sleeper. I sang a lot to him from birth – I made up words about anything to popular tunes. From about 6 months he began to *repeat the tunes perfectly to me. This became his 'party piece' and his repertoire grew. He had a perfect ear. He still detects if I play a wrong note on the piano when he's upstairs on the computer. I would invent rhymes going up and down stairs etc. It always made life fun and happy and helps learning.*

Hush-a-bye, don't you cry

CD TRACK 53

TRADITIONAL AMERICAN LULLABY

Hush-a-bye, don't you cry   Go   to sleep little ba- by.   When you wake,

you shall have cake And all   the pretty little   hor- ses   Black and bay,   dapple and grey

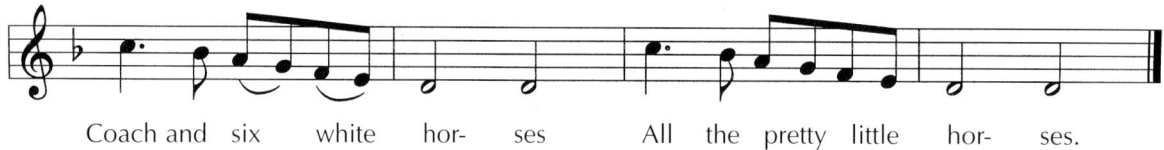

Coach and six   white   hor- ses   All   the pretty little   hor- ses.

Hush-a-bye, don't you cry
Go to sleep little baby.
When you wake, you shall have cake
And all the pretty little horses
Black and bay, dapple and grey
Coach and six white horses
All the pretty little horses.

Wee Willie Winkie

CD TRACK 54

TRADITIONAL SCOTTISH

Wee Willie Win- kie   runs through the town Up- stairs and down- stairs in his night- gown

Rapping at the window, crying through the lock,   Are the children all in bed, for now it's eight o'clock?

Wee Willie Winkie runs through the town
Upstairs and downstairs in his nightgown
Rapping at the window, crying through the lock,
Are the children all in bed, for now it's eight o'clock?

Bye, baby bunting

CD TRACK 55

TRADITIONAL ENGLISH

Bye,   ba- by   bun- ting,   Daddy's gone a- hun- ting   Gone to find a

rab- bit skin To   wrap the ba- by bunt- ing in;   Bye, ba- by   bun- ting.

Bye, baby bunting,
Daddy's gone a-hunting
Gone to find a rabbit skin
To wrap the baby bunting in;
Bye, baby bunting.

Hush little baby

CD TRACK 56

Sing in a swinging style

TRADITIONAL ENGLISH/AMERICAN

Hush little baby, don't say a word, Mamma's gonna buy you a mocking bird.

Hush little baby, don't say a word,
Mamma's gonna buy you a mocking bird.
If that mocking bird won't sing,
Mamma's gonna buy you a diamond ring.
If that diamond ring turns brass,
Mamma's gonna buy you a looking glass.
If that looking glass gets broke,
Mamma's gonna buy you a billy goat.
If that billy goat won't pull,
Mamma's gonna buy you a cart and bull.
If that cart and bull turn over,
Mamma's gonna buy you a dog named Rover.
If that dog named Rover don't bark,
Mamma's gonna buy you a horse and cart.
If that horse and cart fall down,
You'll still be the prettiest baby in town.

When they were children my dad and his brother, who shared a bed, would put their heads under the covers when they were not ready to sleep and play 'Brass Bands', imitating all the instruments.

To get Annie to sleep, I made up a kind of chant saying, 'Say goodnight to...' and I would go through all her family and friends, animals, toys.

We would walk around the bedroom singing a made-up rhyme that got quieter as we went, saying goodnight to each familiar object or picture:

Say good night to the table
Say good night to the chair
Say good night to the rabbit
Say good night to the hare...etc

Hush-a-baw birdie

CD TRACK 57

TRADITIONAL SCOTTISH

Hush- a-baw birdie, croon, croon, Hush- a-baw birdie,

croon, The sheep are gane to the silver wood, And the

cows are gane to the broom, broom, And it's braw milking the kye,

kye, And it's braw milking the kye, The birds are singing, the

bells are ringing, The wild deer come gal- lop- ing by, by.

1. Hush-a-baw birdie, croon, croon,
   Hush-a-baw birdie, croon,
   The sheep are gane to the silver wood,
   And the cows are gane to the broom, broom,
   And it's braw milking the kye, kye,
   And it's braw milking the kye,
   The birds are singing, the bells are ringing,
   The wild deer come galloping by, by.

2. And hush-a-baw birdie, croon, croon,
   Hush-a-baw birdie, croon,
   The gaits are gane to the mountain high,
   And they'll no be hame till noon, noon
   And it's braw milking the kye, kye,
   And it's braw milking the kye,
   The birds are singing, the bells are ringing,
   The wild deer come galloping by, by...
           ...till the child is asleep...

(*braw* = fine, *gaits* = goats, *hame* = home)

Birdies in their nest

Birdies in their nest,   one and two and three,   Under Mother's breast,   warm as warm can be.

Mother keeps you warm, Father brings you food, You've no troubles yet, happy little brood.

Birdies in their nest, one and two and three,
Under Mother's breast, warm as warm can be.
Mother keeps you warm, Father brings you food,
You've no troubles yet, happy little brood.

Mind you do not fall from your nest so high
You've no feathers yet and you cannot fly,
When your feathers grow, on a summer's day,
You will learn to fly, fly, fly away.

*My sister and I used to love it as
children when this song was sung
to us by Edith, our grandmother's
parlour maid in London. I can't
help crying on the last line.*

Bye-sey, bye-sey baby

Bye-sey,   bye-sey   ba-   by,   Bye- sey, bye- sey   bye.

Bye- sey, bye- sey   ba-   by,   Bye- sey, bye- sey   bye.

Bye-sey, bye-sey baby, Bye-sey, bye-sey bye.
Bye-sey, bye-sey baby, Bye-sey, bye-sey bye.

*This song was sung to me as a child. You go on
singing or humming it till the child is asleep.*

Go to sleep, go to sleep

TRADITIONAL AMERICAN

Go to sleep, go to sleep, Go to sleep little ba- by.

When you wake you shall have A coach and six little horses, Five little

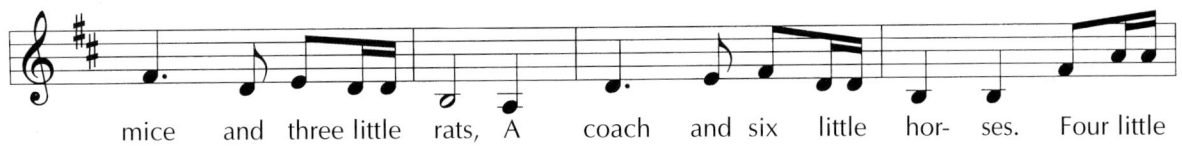

mice and three little rats, A coach and six little hor- ses. Four little

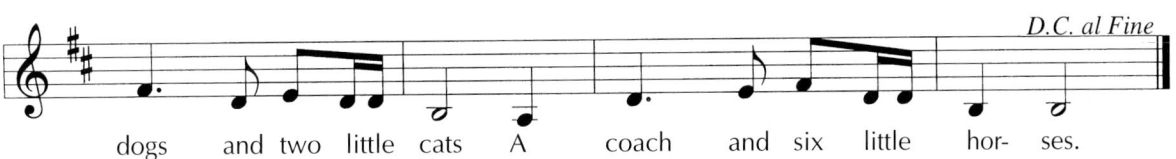

dogs and two little cats A coach and six little hor- ses.

Go to sleep, go to sleep,
Go to sleep little baby.
When you wake you shall have
A coach and six little horses,
Five little mice and three little rats,
A coach and six little horses.
Four little dogs and two little cats
A coach and six little horses.
Go to sleep, go to sleep,
Go to sleep little baby.

I include this song as an example of a lullaby
that expresses a mother's ambivalent feelings.

Oh can ye sew cushions?

CD TRACK 61

TRADITIONAL SCOTTISH

Oh can ye sew cushions, and can ye sew sheets, And

can ye sing ba- la- loo when my bonnie greets? And hee and baw

bir- die, and hee and baw lamb, And hee and baw bir- die my

CHORUS

bon- nie wee lamb. Hee- o, haw- o, what'll I do with you?

Black's the life that I lead with you. Man- y of you;

lit- tle to give you, Hee- o, haw- o, what'll I do with you?

1. Oh can ye sew cushions, and can ye sew sheets,
   And can ye sing balaloo when my bonnie greets?
   And hee and baw birdie, and hee and baw lamb,
   And hee and baw birdie my bonnie wee lamb.

CHORUS
   Hee-o, haw-o, what'll I do with you?
   Black's the life that I lead with you.
   Many of you; little to give you,
   Hee-o, haw-o, what'll I do with you?

2. Now hush-a-by lammie, and hush-a-by dear,
   Now hush-a-by lammie, your mother is here.
   And the wild wind is raving, your mother's heart's sore.
   The wild wind is raving, but you care no more.

3. Sing balaloo lammie, sing balaloo dear,
   Does wee lammie know that its daddy's not here?
   You're rocking quite sweetly on mother's warm knee,
   But daddy's a-rocking upon the salt sea.

Home, home on the range

CD TRACK 62

Home, home on the range Where the deer and the antelope play And

seldom is heard a dis- paraging word And the cows come home happy each day.

Home, home on the range
Where the deer and the antelope play
And seldom is heard a disparaging word
And the cows come home happy each day.

Daisies

CD TRACK 63

WORDS: FRANK D. SHERMAN

MUSIC: WINIFRED DYROFF

At evening when I go to bed, I see the stars shine o-ver my head; They are the lit-tle dai-sies white That dot the mead-ow of the night.

At evening when I go to bed,
I see the stars shine over my head;
They are the little daisies white
That dot the meadow of the night.

And often while I'm dreaming so,
Across the sky the Moon will go,
It is a lady sweet and fair,
Who comes to gather daisies there.

For when at morning I arise,
There's not a star left in the skies;
She's picked them all and dropped them down
Into the meadows of the town.

76

Too-ra-loo-ra, loo-ra-loo-ra baby

CD TRACK 64

Too- ra- loo- ra,   loo- ra- loo- ra   ba-   by

Do   you want the   moon   to   play   with   Or the

stars   to   run   a-   way   with.

1. Too-ra-loo-ra, loo-ra-loo-ra baby
   Do you want the moon to play with
   Or the stars to run away with.

2. Too-ra-loo-ra loo-ra-loo-ra bye-byes,
   Won't you close your sleepy eye-eyes
   Byesy byesy bye-byes.

Golden slumbers

CD TRACK 65

TRADITIONAL ENGLISH

Gol- den slum- bers kiss your eyes, Smiles a-

wake you when you rise; Sleep, pret- ty

mai- den, do not cry, And I will

sing a lul- la- by. Lul- la- by,

lul- la- by, lul- la- by.

Golden slumbers kiss your eyes,
Smiles awake you when you rise;
Sleep, pretty maiden*, do not cry,
And I will sing a lullaby.
Lullaby, lullaby, lullaby.

Care you know not, therefore sleep
While I o'er you watch do keep;
Sleep, pretty darling*, do not cry,
And I will sing a lullaby.
Lullaby, lullaby, lullaby.

* Use 'my darling' if you want instead, or for a boy.

The song I remember most clearly from my childhood was 'Golden Slumbers' sung as a lullaby whenever I had had a difficult day, or was having trouble getting to sleep. When I hear it now I always feel comforted. And of course, it is naturally the song I sang to my own two children as a bedtime lullaby when they were very young. Even now, at seven and eight years old, they still like it if they are troubled for any reason. I always remember my mother stroking my forehead as she sang it to me and I do exactly the same to my children.

Go to sleep my baby

Go to sleep my baby
Close your pretty eyes
Angels up above you
Whispering lullabies.
Great big moon is shining
Stars begin to peep
It's time for little *Peter*
To go to sleep
(hum)
Time for *Peter* to go to sleep.

Many parents have told me of the comfort that talking of angels brings their children. Here are some songs personal to different families.

I'll sing you a little song

WORDS AND MUSIC: JILL NEWSOME

I'll sing you a little song And it won't take very long
The stars in the sky Look down where you lie

Good night, my darling good-night.
They shine so bright for you.

CHORUS
Snuggle up, little dar-ling, snuggle up

The ang-els will guard you Will guard you, will guard you.

All through the night.

I'll sing you a little song
And it won't take very long
Good night, my darling goodnight.

The stars in the sky
Look down where you lie
They shine so bright for you.

CHORUS
    Snuggle up, little darling, snuggle up
    The angels will guard you
    Will guard you, will guard you.
    All through the night.

In the field, in the town,
The silver moon is looking down
At you safe fast asleep tonight.

CHORUS

*I sang this to my girls, making up as many
verses as it took to get them to sleep. As they fell
asleep, the softness of my voice changed
accordingly. The words and tune were
improvised, as need be.*

Go to sleep my love

WORDS AND MUSIC: JULIET GRANGER

Go   to sleep my   baby   Go   to sleep my   love

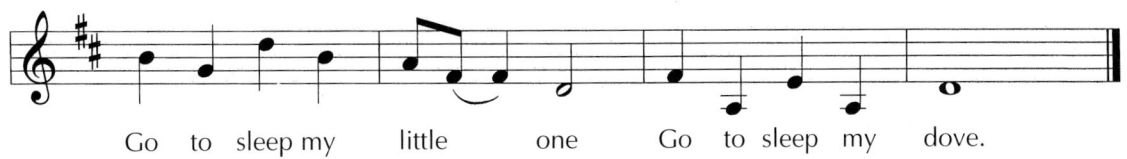

Go   to sleep my   little   one   Go   to sleep my   dove.

Go to sleep my baby
Go to sleep my love
Go to sleep my little one
Go to sleep my dove.

Mama's right beside you now
Dada's right here too
The angels are all around you now
Sending all their love to you.

Go to sleep my little boy
Go to sleep my love
Go to sleep my little one
Go to sleep my joy.

Jim would hum Irish ballads e.g. Planxty Irwin, walking around with a tearful baby. It helped him gently pace up and down to the rhythm and it soothed the baby to sleep.
2-4 years: we sang songs about angels keeping them safe. Repeating the song would always relax them and they would soon be drifting off to sleep. Iona sings it to her dolls to make them feel 'comfy inside'. The song was as much part of the bedtime routine as brushing teeth. It gives her a nice feeling. It symbolises a cosy safe bed with Mum or Dad beside them as reassurance. They can hear the voice as they float to sleep.

Sleep like a lady

CD TRACK 69

WORDS AND MUSIC: JULIE HARDING

Bye, bye my baby,
Sleep like a lady.
You shall have milkie
When the cows come home.
When the cows come home my dear,
You'll have milk to give good cheer;
Milk to drink and cheese to eat,
Lucky little lady.
Night, night sweetheart,
See you in the morning.
Sleep tight baby,
Day-time will soon be dawning.

Some lullabies in different languages

As well as rooting children within their own culture, singing also has a valuable part to play in fostering an appreciation of other cultures and awakening children to the wider human world, to its diversity and richness. Young children are so open and accepting that they drink in 'foreign' words as easily as those from their own language.

O ba, o ba

CD TRACK 70

GAELIC

O   ba,   o   ba,   o   ba,   o   i   O   ba,   o   ba,   o   ba,   o   i   O

ba,   o   ba,   o   ba,   o   i   Cha   bhi   mi   'gad   thaladh   Bho'n   sharaich   thu   mi.

O ba, o ba, o ba, o i
O ba, o ba, o ba, o i
O ba, o ba, o ba, o i

Cha bhi mi 'gad thaladh
Bho'n sharaich thu mi.

Approximate phonetic pronounciation:
Ha vi mi gad hala
Von shara tu mi.

Translation:
O ba, o ba, o ba, o i,
I will not rock you to sleep,
Since you have worn me out.

*From South Uist, Outer Hebrides. Given by
Miss Peigi Macrae, North Glendale, who
described it as the sleepiest song she knew.*

83

Night is here

CD TRACK 71

CHEROKEE

Night is here, ay a ha. Stars appear, ay a ha. Mamama, ay a ha.

Night is here, ay a ha.
Stars appear, ay a ha.
Mamama, ay a ha.

Owls you hear, ay a ha.
Do not fear, ay a ha.
Mamama, ay a ha.

Close your eyes, ay a ha.
Go to sleep, ay a ha.
Mamama, ay a ha.

Aja tutaja

CD TRACK 72

SLOVENIAN

A- ja tu- ta- ja Zib- ka se ma- ja

No- tri v tej zib- ki Si- nek moj spi.

Aja tutaja
Zibka se maja
Notri v tej zibki
Sinek moj spi.

You can put the name of the child in the last line:
   Mary moja spi.
   Jamie moj spi.

Translation:
Aja tutaja,
The cradle is swinging,
Inside the cradle
My little son sleeps.

Oto omo mi oto

NIGERIAN

O- to   o- mo   mi   o- to   Se- bi mo- ti   be   o   le-   kan

O   da   bi   o   l'a- se-   ju   l'o-   wo

Oto omo mi oto
Sebi moti be o lekan
O da bi o l'aseju l'owo

Translation:
Oh my child stop crying,
I've appeased you,
I've begged you.
You are exaggerating your condition.

I once worked in a nursery for children with multiple special needs. Leanne was a two-year-old with Retts syndrome. She used to cry and scream a lot when I first worked there. I'd sing her 'Twinkle Twinkle', and 'Baa Baa Black Sheep', and 'Lara's theme' (from Dr. Zhivago) over and over again, and it stopped her screaming. She'd smile and calm down. I think if I went back now, 4 years later and sang her those songs, her eyes would light up.

I would sing to sleep babies with Down's syndrome. It's so important to repeat the songs until they are well known to the children. Sometimes I would chant 'Om' and get them to touch my throat, to feel the vibrations.

Fais dodo

FRENCH

Fais do-do, Co-lin mon petit frè-re; Fais do-do, Tu au-

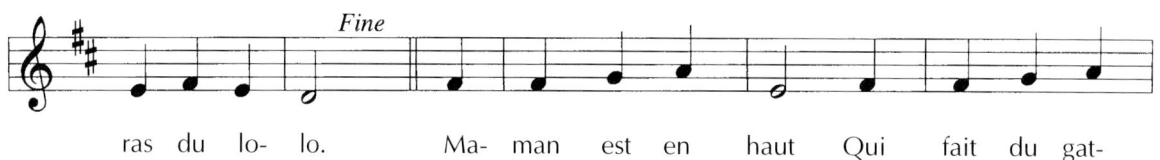

ras du lo-lo. Ma-man est en haut Qui fait du gat-

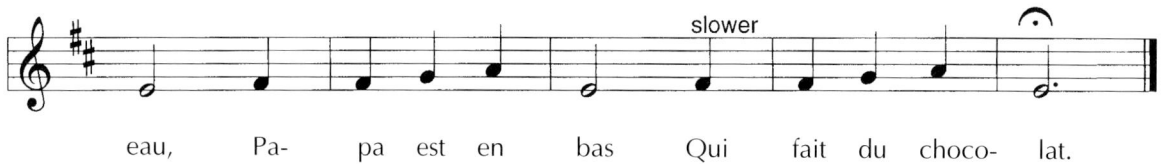

eau, Pa-pa est en bas Qui fait du choco-lat.

CHORUS
    Fais dodo,
    Colin mon petit frère;
    Fais dodo,
    Tu auras du lolo.

Maman est en haut
Qui fait du gateau,
Papa est en bas
Qui fait du chocolat.

CHORUS

Papa est en haut,
Qui prend son repos,
Maman est en bas,
Qui prend son repas.

CHORUS

Translation:
    Go to sleep.
    Colin my little brother;
    Go to sleep,
    You will have some milk.

Mummy is upstairs,
Making a cake,
Daddy is downstairs
Making chocolate.

Daddy is upstairs
Taking a nap,
Mummy is downstairs,
Eating her meal.

La la sana la la

ZULU

La   la sa-   na   la   la   Wey'm   shel   wa-   ne

Ksa   sa um-ga-be-   le   Wey'm   shel   wa-   ne

La la sana la la
Wey'm shel wane
Ksa sa umgabele
Wey'm shel wane

Rough translation:
Sleep baby,
sleep my child,
tomorrow we will go my child.

My daughter aged six has been waking up every night for weeks now. I sang this song to her a few nights ago for the first time. She has asked for it every night since and it works every time! It seems to have an instantly relaxing and soporific effect. She slides onto the pillow, closes her eyes and is very drowsy by the time I have sung it five times.

Prayers

Saying or singing prayers gives comfort to children, whether they come from a religious family or not. Children are naturally religious, through their innate wonder at the world, and prayers can enfold them in a sense of trust and security.

We sang a special song for each of our children at their christening, and it has remained as their bedtime song ever since. They know it as their own special song.

God sufficeth

CD TRACK 76

BAHAI

God suf- fi- ceth All things a- bove all things, And noth- ing in the

Heavens or the Earth But God suf- fi- ceth. Ve- ri- ly He is in Him- self the

Knower, Sus- tainer, the Om- ni- po- tent.

God sufficeth
All things above all things,
And nothing in the Heavens or the earth
But God sufficeth.
Verily He is in Himself the Knower,
Sustainer, the Omnipotent.

Can be sung as a 3 part round (see note on page xxi).

I worked at Mother Teresa's centres in Delhi and Calcutta, where some babies were too weak to live. I would hold the dying baby close, touching my skin. They would suck my skin and I would sing and croon to them. They were very, very peaceful. I'm sure they felt my love for them. You could feel them ebbing away very gently, with no distress, no crying.

O God guide me

CD TRACK 77

BAHAI

O God guide me, Protect me Il- lumine the lamp of my heart, And

make it a brilliant star. Thou art the might- y, The power- ful.

O God guide me,
Protect me
Illumine the lamp of my heart,
And make it a brilliant star.
Thou art the mighty,
The powerful.

Same prayer in French
O Dieu guide moi,
Protège moi,
Illumine la lampe de mon coeur,
Et fais moi une étoile brillante.
Tu es le fort,
Le tout puissant.

*I'd sing 'Oh God guide me, protect me', while
Joel was in the womb – he'd kick, and then I
knew he was still alive! Which was very
important to me as I'd had three babies die in
the womb before. The effect of singing was also
evident at his birth. I had the planned
Caesarean with an epidural and was awake.
The anaesthetist said, 'Give baby to Mother to
kiss'. My baby was crying fiercely, and I sang
'Oh God guide me and protect me', at which
point he stopped crying and was totally calm.
He was just against my cheek as the operation
was still going on.*

May the longtime sun shine on you

CELTIC

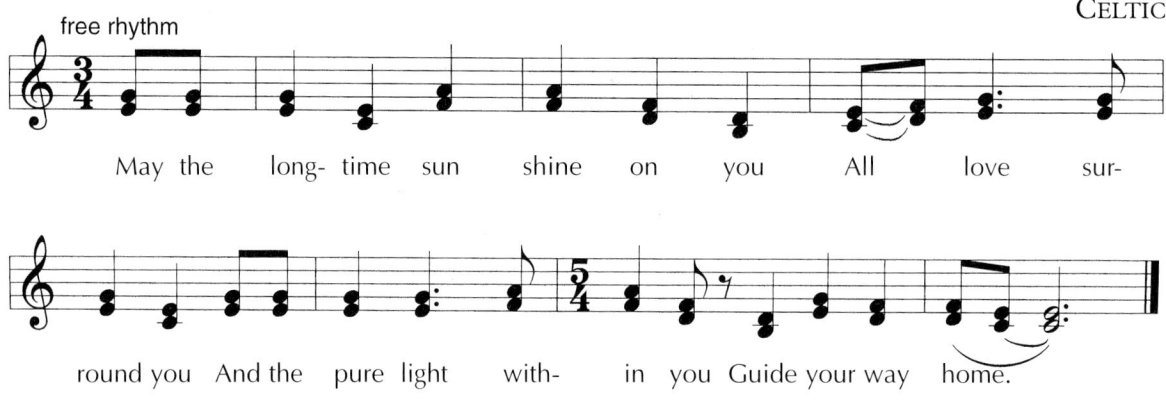

May the longtime sun shine on you
All love surround you
And the pure light within you
Guide your way home.

Matthew, Mark, Luke and John,
Bless the bed that I lie on.
Four corners to my bed,
Four angels round me spread;
One at my head, one at my feet
And two at my heart, my soul to keep.

Alternatively:
Four corners to my bed
Four angels to my head
Two to watch and one to pray
And one to keep bad dreams away.

Songs for Special Occasions

Birth of a brother or sister

My new little sister is small

CD TRACK 79

WORDS AND MUSIC: CANDY VERNEY

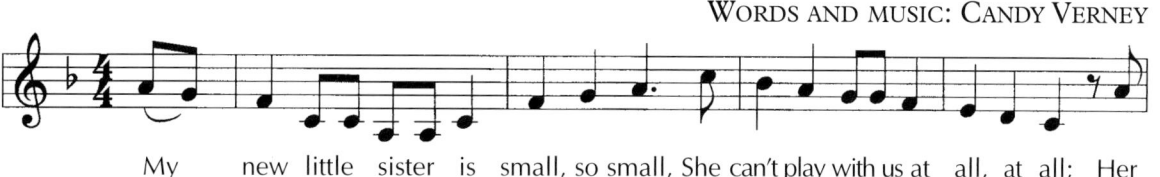

My new little sister is small, so small, She can't play with us at all, at all; Her

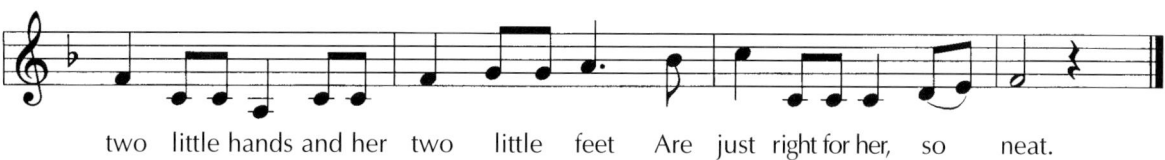

two little hands and her two little feet Are just right for her, so neat.

My new little sister is small, so small,
She can't play with us at all, at all;
Her two little hands and her two little feet
Are just right for her, so neat.

Sometimes she wakes me when she cries in the night,
And sometimes she cries as well in the day,
Then Mummy feeds her and lays her to sleep.
When she's much bigger we'll play.

Illness or upset

Singing regulates, sustains and deepens the breath, increases the sensitivity of the auditory system and refines the internal sensing process. Singing can resonate the entire physical body and electro-magnetic field, fully engage the mind, give the emotions a vehicle for expression and produce an overall sense of wellbeing. When we combine the singing of sustained pitches with specific vowels and directed concentration we can, in addition, revitalise our organs, tone our endocrine gland system and calm our nervous system. In short, the quality of our voice can be a reflection of our emotional, physical, and spiritual condition – our health.

RANDALL MCCLELLAN
in *The Healing Forces of Music*

Bimbole Baggins, what are we to do?
Bimbole Baggins in a terrible stew.

When Polly was small I used to sing this ditty to her. It went with a rocking motion and was used when she was upset. 'The thing that interests me now looking back, is that it was recognition of the upset. We have a problem, sometimes, with allowing negative experience and acknowledging it.

If Ben is distressed or unhappy about something, and I have an inkling what that is, I make up a song about it, always ending with the problem sorted:

Ben went to play to his friend's house
We went to his friend's today.
They played and played and played and played
They didn't stop all day.
But then they got cross and upset
And they began to fight.
If their mums hadn't stopped them
They would have fought all night.
But I think that Ben was very, very tired
And that next time he sees his friend,
Everything will be all right.

This seems to work much better than a lecture! It eases the pressure of the moment and even relaxes them into listening and understanding their problem, when it seems they never will. Kind of removing them from themselves. Sometimes I have to sing for ages. But it actually makes the whole problem easier for me too, and helps me to understand as best I can.

I found this song (see below) particularly useful when working with disturbed children. The water element can carry you and make things flow. Why is it so good? It is forming a relationship with a rhythm. You need a simple melody, lots of repetition, and gradual change. It builds order and harmony in the child.

I love to row my big blue boat

CD TRACK 80

TRADITIONAL ENGLISH

I love to row in my big blue boat, big blue boat, big blue boat, I

love to row in my big blue boat, Out on the deep blue sea.

For a child who cannot concentrate, or is over-active: Sit on the floor, facing the child, hold child's hands in yours.

I love to row in my big blue boat, big blue boat, big blue boat,
I love to row in my big blue boat,
Out on the deep blue sea.

My big blue boat has two white sails, two white sails, two white sails,
My big blue boat has two white sails
Out on the deep blue sea. *(arms up and out, describing sail)*

Other verses:

My big blue boat has a flag on top... *(make up actions)*
My big blue boat hits a rock...
The water comes in right over my head...
We sink right down to the bottom of the sea...
We swim very hard right to the top...
And now our feet are on the land...

When I was a nurse in a children's ward, I used to sing to the children when they were ill or frightened. It always calmed them. It broke the pattern of their fears, and they felt reassured. I felt very embarrassed because it wasn't usual for nurses to sing, and I haven't got a voice, but I did it because it comforted them and they loved it.

In the hospital where I worked, there was a baby dying in intensive care. The parents brought their older son in to say goodbye. The little boy spontaneously touched the baby and sang to him. From that moment the baby started to fight for life, and he made a complete recovery.

When my daughter was hospitalised in Italy, with severely restricted movement, singing was a regular part of the hospital routine, to exercise the children's lungs and breathing.

Joel suffered a lot from earache and Glue Ear. I found singing soothed him. We would sing Lara's theme from Doctor Zhivago, or 'Go to sleep my baby'.

When they were very young and got ill, their favourite song usually comforted them the best. Each child had a different one; through singing every night at bedtime you soon find out which song is best-loved.

I have a memory from the 1940's of my brother and me with towels round our necks gargling with salty water, to the tune of 'God save the King' .

Be kind to one another
And every living thing
The fishes in the water
The birds upon the wing.

Birthdays

Some birthday rounds:

See note on page xxi.

Joyful, joyful, joyful greetings

CD TRACK 81

WORDS AND MUSIC: KENNETH GREENYER

Joy- ful, joy- ful, joy- ful greet- ings We

come to wish you everything Of good the com- ing year may bring

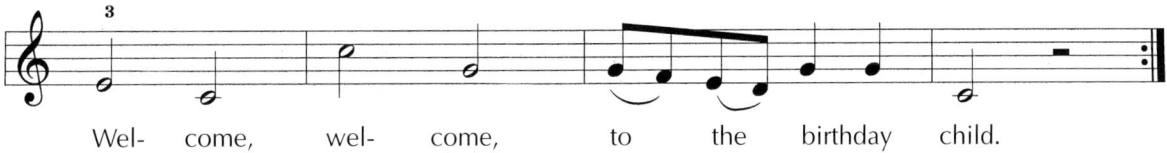

Wel- come, wel- come, to the birthday child.

Joyful, joyful, joyful greetings
We come to wish you everything
Of good the coming year may bring
Welcome, welcome, to the birthday child.

To you we sing

CD TRACK 82

To you we sing
And birthday greetings bring
To celebrate your birth,
An angel here on earth.

Now we will wish you many happy returns

CD TRACK 83

Now we will wish you many happy returns
And the best of love for your birthday.

We wish you a happy birthday

CD TRACK 84

We wish you a happy birthday
A joyful and happy birthday
To you dear *John*...
We wish you a long, long life.

A verse for the night before the birthday

When I have said my evening prayer,
And my clothes are folded on the chair,
And mother switches off the light,
I'll still be ___ years old tonight.
But, from the very break of day,
Before the children rise and play,
Before the darkness turns to gold
Tomorrow, I'll be ___ years old.
___ kisses when I wake,
___ candles on my cake.

Dancing / party games

At children's parties we always had lots of singing games and circle songs e.g. 'Ring o' roses', 'I sent a letter to my love', 'Sleep the dragon'. The children always wanted to join in and all enjoyed it. It made the party atmosphere happy and calm, not wild.

Sally go round the sun

CD TRACK 85

TRADITIONAL ENGLISH

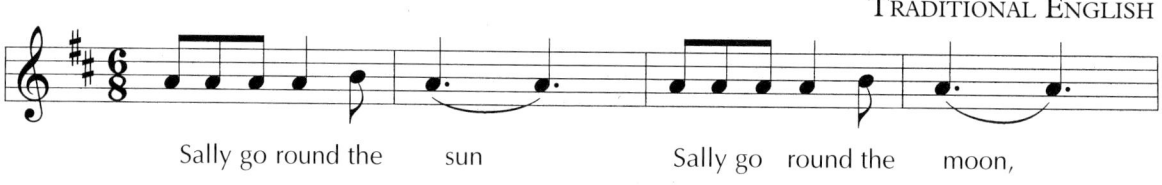

Sally go round the sun   Sally go round the moon,

Sally go round the chimney pots On a Saturday af- ter- noon.

Sally go round the sun
Sally go round the moon,
Sally go round the chimney pots
On a Saturday afternoon.

Hold hands in a ring, dance round in a circle. At end of rhyme, bump bottoms with your neighbour on one side, then the other – alternatively, with very little ones, you can lift them up.
Repeat the song, circling round the other way.

Jack be nimble, Jack be quick,
Jack jump over the candlestick.

Hold hands in a ring, very still, expectant. Then on 'over', jump as high as you can.

100

Follow my leader to London Town

CD TRACK 86

TRADITIONAL ENGLISH

Follow my leader to London Town, London Town, London Town

Follow my leader to London Town, So early in the morning.

Follow my leader to London Town, London Town, London Town
Follow my leader to London Town,
So early in the morning.

Someone is the leader, everybody follows in a long line, imitating the actions.

Other verses:

Hopping along to London Town, sliding, jumping,
backwards, crawling etc

Now we've arrived at London Town, London Town, London Town
Now we've arrived at London Town
We sit and have an ice cream.

Jump high *(legs up)*
Jump low *(little jump)*
Touch the sky *(jump with arms up)*
And the earth below *(crouch down)*
Jump out wide *(arms and legs wide)*
Jump in narrow *(arms and legs narrow)*
Hands to the ground *(child puts his hands on the ground)*
I'm a wheelbarrow. *(adult lifts up his legs – the child can
then walk on his hands.*

CANDY VERNEY

Here we go round the mulberry bush

CD TRACK 87

TRADITIONAL ENGLISH

Here we go round the mul- berry bush, The mul-berry bush, the mul- berry bush,

Here we go round the mul- berry bush On a cold and fros- ty morn- ing.

Here we go round the mulberry bush,
The mulberry bush, the mulberry bush,
Here we go round the mulberry bush
On a cold and frosty morning.

Other verses:

This is the way we wash our face, brush our teeth, stamp on the ground etc

I remember my Grandma singing 'Here we go round the mulberry bush' with me. In her garden she had a willow tree. She was full of fun, and me and my sister and my grandma used to skip around that tree, singing 'Mulberry Bush'. I really loved her more than anyone else. She was always telling us stories. I think that's why we loved her so much.

To the tune of *Mulberry Bush*.

Who'll come into my wee ring,
My wee ring, my wee ring,
Who'll come into my wee ring,
And make it a little bit bigger?

Sur le pont d'Avignon l'on y danse, l'on y danse, *(dance in a ring)*
Sur le pont d'Avignon l'on y danse, tout en rond.

Les mesdames font comme ça *(all curtsy)*
Et puis encore comme ça.

Sur le pont d'Avignon l'on y danse, l'on y danse,
Sur le pont d'Avignon l'on y danse, tout en rond.

Les messieurs font comme ça *(all bow)*
Et puis encore comme ça.

Sur le pont d'Avignon l'on y danse, l'on y danse,
Sur le pont d'Avignon l'on y danse, tout en rond.

Translation:
On the bridge of Avignon,
we dance in a round.
The women go like this / the men go like this.

C'era una casa

C'era una ca- sa tanta car- in- a   Senza sof- fi- to,   senza cu- ci- na
Non si po- te- va   entrare   dentro   Perche non c'e- ra   il pavi-   men- to.

Non si po- te- va   fa- re pi- pi   Perche non c'e- ra il   va- si- no   li.

Ma e- ra bel- la,   bella dav- ve- ro   In via dei Mat- ti,   numero   ze- ro.

An action song from Italy★

C'era una casa tanta carina (*make square in air*)
Senza soffito, senza cucina (*finger tips together to make ceiling, stir pan*)
Non si poteva entrare dentro (*open door*)
Perche non c'era il pavimento. (*hand flat indicating floor*)
Non si poteva fare pipi (*squat down*)
Perche non c'era il vasino li. (*round shape with hands*)
Ma era bella, bella davvero
In via dei Matti, numero zero.

Translation:
There was a pretty house
Without a ceiling, without a kitchen.
You couldn't go in
As there was no floor.
You couldn't do a wee
Because there was no potty.
But it was beautiful, truly beautiful,
In Crazy St, number zero.

★ 'c' is pronounced 'ch', except in 'carina'
where it is pronounced 'k'; and 'ch' is
pronounced 'k'

I'm very, very small

CD TRACK 90

I'm very, very small, and I'm very, very tall, Sometimes small and

sometimes tall, Which shall I be now... Tall!

I'm very, very small, and I'm very, very tall,
Sometimes small and sometimes tall,
Which shall I be now...Tall!

*Do actions, each time ask a different child either
to be small or tall.*

Pease porridge hot

CD TRACK 91

TRADITIONAL ENGLISH

Pease porridge hot,   Pease porridge cold, Pease porridge in the pot, Nine days old.
Some like it hot,   Some like it cold,   Some like it in the pot,   Nine days old.

Pease porridge hot,
Pease porridge cold,
Pease porridge in the pot
Nine days old.
Some like it hot,
Some like it cold,
Some like it in the pot
Nine days old.

*Everybody puts their hands in a pile one on top
of the other. Then draw them out one at a time
from the bottom, in time with the song, and
place back on top.*

Train is a-comin' oh yes

WORDS AND MUSIC: ESTHER L. NELSON

Train is a-com-in' oh yes, Train is a-com-in' oh yes,

Train is a- com-in' Train is a- com-in' Train is a- com-in' oh yes.

Train is a-comin' oh yes,
Train is a-comin' oh yes,
Train is a-comin'
Train is a-comin'
Train is a-comin' oh yes.

Better get your ticket, oh yes,
Better get your ticket, oh yes,
Better get your ticket
Better get your ticket
Better get your ticket, oh yes.

A train song, where children form a line, each child holding onto the one in front.

An adult or older child is the 'engine', and very slowly in time to the song, chugs around the room.

Before the train takes off, lift your hand, pull the bell and do a train whistle. Pull the bell again and this is the start of the song.

When I was little I made up a song for queuing (cinema in mind I think) which has gone down in my family history. It was the words that people liked:

Standing in the queue with Stanley
Ooh he looks ever so manly
While all the crowd around us bustles
I just look at his muscles.

It's quite fun for children to make up other verses:

Standing in the queue with Fred
I just wish I were dead…

Darnell is a jumping bean

CD TRACK 93
MUSIC: CANDY VERNEY

Darnell is a jumping bean The jumpiest bean you've ever seen,

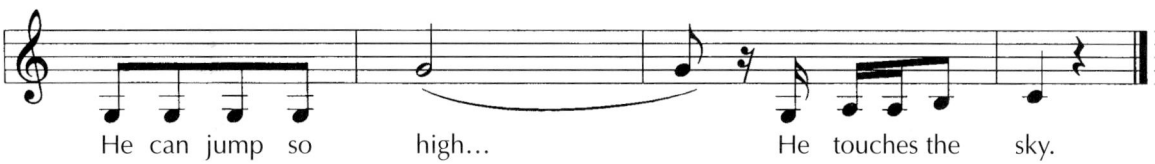

He can jump so high... He touches the sky.

Darnell is a jumping bean
The jumpiest bean you've ever seen,
He can jump so high...
He touches the sky.

Clap up high

CD TRACK 94

MUSIC: CANDY VERNEY

Clap up high,   clap down low   Hop a- round like a   big black crow.

Clap up high,   clap down low,   Run a- round on   tip- py   toe.

Clap up high, clap down low
Hop around like a big black crow.
Clap up high, clap down low,
Run around on tippy toe.

Last evening Cousin Peter came

CD TRACK 95

TRADITIONAL ENGLISH

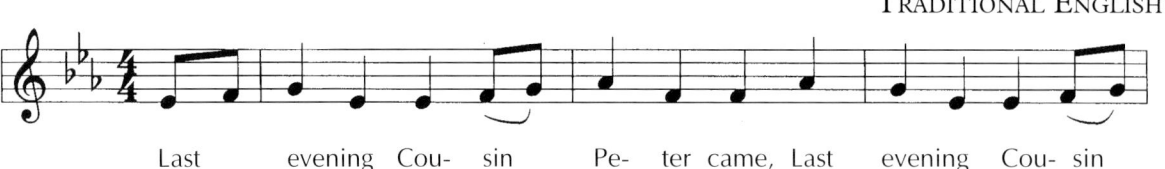

Last   evening Cou- sin   Pe- ter came, Last   evening   Cou- sin

Pe- ter came, Last   evening Cou- sin   Pe- ter came, To show that he was   here.

Last evening Cousin Peter came,
Last evening Cousin Peter came,
Last evening Cousin Peter came,
To show that he was here.

Other verses:

He wiped his feet upon the mat…
He hung his hat upon the peg…
He kicked his shoes off one by one…
He danced about in stockinged feet…
He played he was a big brown bear…
He tossed us up into the air…
He bowed to us and said Goodbye…

Stand in a ring and copy Cousin Peter.

See the ponies galloping

CD TRACK 96

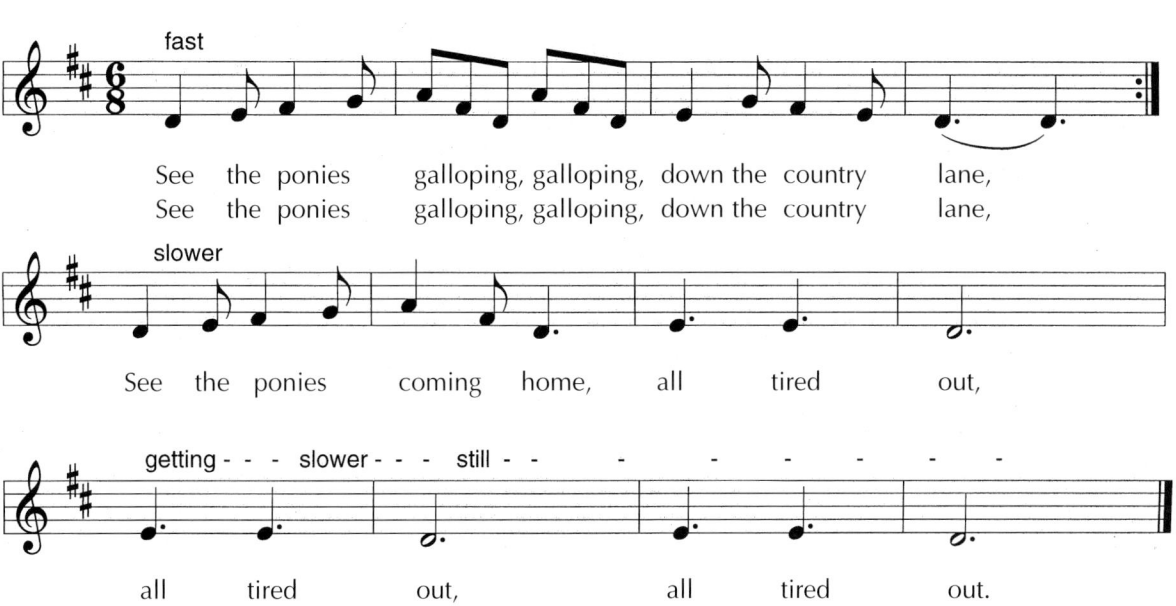

See the ponies galloping, galloping, down the country lane, *(gallop around room)*
See the ponies galloping, galloping, down the country lane,
See the ponies galloping, galloping, down the country lane,
See the ponies galloping, galloping, down the country lane,

See the ponies coming home, all tired out, all tired out, all tired out. *(slow down, and come
to sit together in centre of room*

A good song for calming down and bringing everyone together.

We've sung our songs and clapped our hands

CD TRACK 97

We've sung our songs and clapped our hands
And danced our way through many lands.
It's time to hold together our hands
Goodbye everybody goodbye.

Goodbye now, until we meet again

CD TRACK 98

Goodbye now, goodbye now, until we meet again,
We bow once, we bow twice, until we meet again.

Nonsense verse for any occasion

Rhymes free the fancy, charm tongue and ear,
delight the inward eye.

WALTER DE LA MARE

One, two three o-leerie

TRADITIONAL

One,   two   three o-   leerie   I   spy   Mrs   Gearly

Sitting on a   basket cheerie   Eating   baby's chocolate   Eating chocolate babies.

One, two three o-leerie
I spy Mrs Gearly
Sitting on a basket cheerie
Eating baby's chocolate
Eating chocolate babies.

Originally a ball game, but could be adapted
to all sorts of games.

Great A, little a *(slowly)*
Bouncing B,
The cat's in the cupboard *(fast)*
And can't catch me.

If all the world was paper
And all the sea was ink,
If all the trees were bread and cheese,
What should we have to drink?

Here comes the Boys Brigade,
All covered in marmalade.
A tuppenny ha'penny pillbox
And half a yard of braid.

Pop! Goes the weasel

Although this is very well known, I include it
as it has a useful rhythm for accompanying
made up games.

CD TRACK 99B

TRADITIONAL

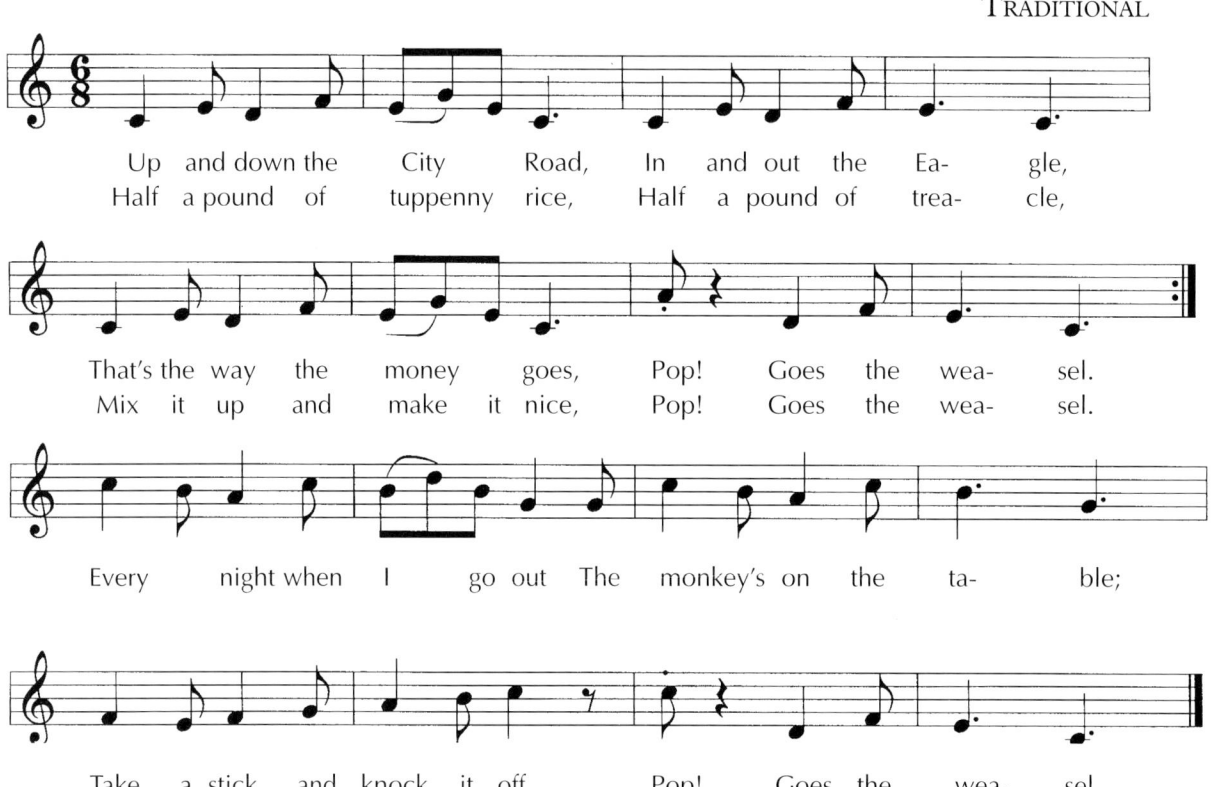

Up   and down the   City   Road,   In   and out   the   Ea-   gle,
Half   a pound   of   tuppenny   rice,   Half   a pound of   trea-   cle,

That's the   way   the   money   goes,   Pop!   Goes   the   wea-   sel.
Mix   it   up   and   make   it   nice,   Pop!   Goes   the   wea-   sel.

Every   night when   I   go   out   The   monkey's   on   the   ta-   ble;

Take   a stick   and   knock   it   off,   Pop!   Goes   the   wea-   sel.

Up and down the City Road,
In and out the Eagle,
That's the way the money goes,
Pop! Goes the weasel.

Half a pound of tuppenny rice,
Half a pound of treacle,
Mix it up and make it nice,
Pop! Goes the weasel.

Every night when I go out
The monkey's on the table;
Take a stick and knock it off,
Pop! Goes the weasel.

Mares eat oats and does eat oats

CD TRACK 99C

Mares eat oats and does eat oats
And little lambs eat ivy,
A kid'll eat ivy too, wouldn't you?

Last line sounds like nonsense when sung at speed!

**Skipping and hopscotch rhyme
from West Yorkshire**

Eeny meeny macaracca
Air I dominacca
Chicka bidda
Lolla poppa
Rum pum push

One two three, mother caught a flea,
Put it in the teapot to make a pot of tea.
The flea jumped out, mother gave a shout
Father came in with his shirt hanging out.

Here am I,
Little Jumping Joan,
When nobody's with me,
I'm all alone.

There was an old woman called Nothing-at-all,
Who lived in a dwelling exceedingly small;
A man stretched his mouth to its utmost extent,
And down at one gulp house and old woman went.

Cock a doodle doo!

CD TRACK **99**D

Cock a doo- dle doo! My dame has lost her shoe, My

mas- ter's lost his fiddling stick, And doesn't know what to do.

Cock a doodle doo!
My dame has lost her shoe,
My master's lost his fiddling stick,
And doesn't know what to do.

There was an old crow

CD TRACK **99**E

NURSERY RHYME

MUSIC: CANDY VERNEY

There was an old crow   Sat upon a clod; That's the end of my song.   That's odd.

There was an old crow
Sat upon a clod;
That's the end of my song.
That's odd.

114

Hokey, pokey, whisky, thum

NURSERY RHYME　　　　　　　　　　　　　　　　　　　MUSIC: CANDY VERNEY

Ho- key, po- key, whis- ky, thum,　How d'you like your po- ta- toes done?

Boiled　in　whisky,　boiled in rum, Says the King of the　Cannibal　Is-　lands.

Hokey, pokey, whisky, thum,
How d'you like potatoes done?
Boiled in whisky, boiled in rum,
Says the King of the Cannibal Islands.

---

*Marion talking to her grandson, about songs they made up
together, and might pass on to me:*

Marion:　What about the Yawning Man?
　Odin:　That's OK
Marion:　What about Wiggly Waggly?
　Odin:　That's OK
Marion:　What about Cowrie Shells?
　Odin:　O nanny, you can't give that away, that's our song!

Counting songs

The age range of this book is too early for
formal learning. But through singing number-
and counting songs, children will learn
effortlessly, 'drinking in' the numbers, and
simply enjoying the repetition and rhymes.

There were ten in the bed

CD TRACK 99G

TRADITIONAL ENGLISH

There were ten in the bed And the little one said, Roll over, Roll

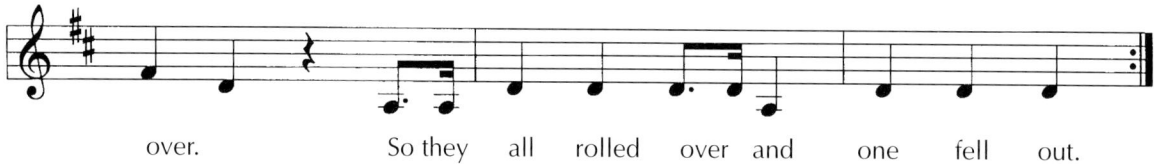

over. So they all rolled over and one fell out.

There were ten in the bed
And the little one said, Roll over, Roll over.
So they all rolled over and one fell out.

There were nine in the bed... etc

One's none;
Two's some;
Three's many;
Four's a penny;
Five's a little hundred.

One, two, buckle my shoe;
Three, four, knock at the door;
Five, six, pick up sticks;
Seven, eight, lay them straight;
Nine, ten, a big fat hen;
Eleven, twelve, dig and delve;
Thirteen, fourteen, maids a-courting;
Fifteen, sixteen, maids in the kitchen;
Seventeen, eighteen, maids in waiting;
Nineteen, twenty, my plate's empty.

Uno, dos, y tres

MEXICAN COUNTING SONG

U- no, dos, y tres, cuatro, cinco, seis, Siete, ocho,

nueve, I can count to diez. La la la... etc

Uno, dos, y tres, cuatro, cinco, seis,
Siete, ocho, nueve, I can count to diez.
La la la...

Ala, mala mink, monk,
Tink, tonk, toozey,
Oozy, voozy, aggardy,
Ah, vah, vack.

One-ery, two-ery, tickery, seven,
Hallibo, crackibo, ten and eleven,
Spin, span, muskidan,
Twiddle-um, twaddle-um, twenty-one.

One-ery, two-ery, ickery, Ann,
Phillisy, phollisy, Nicholas John,
Quever, quaver, Irish Mary,
Stickeram, stackeram, buck.

One, two, three, four, five, six, seven,
All good children go to heaven.
Penny on the water, tuppence on the sea,
Threepence on the railway, and out goes SHE.

Counting cherry stones

Tinker
tailor
soldier
sailor
rich man
poor man
beggar man
thief.

Lady
baby
gypsy
queen.

...wedding

This year
Next year
Sometime
Never.

Coach
Carriage
Wheelbarrow
Dustcart.

Big house
Little house
Pigsty
Barn.

One, two three, four,
Mary at the cottage door,
Five, six, seven, eight,
Eating cherries off a plate.

Bibliography, sources and useful addresses

Music books/sources

Carey, Diana and Large, Judy: *Festivals, Family and Food,* Hawthorn Press, 1982

Hart & Lobel: *Sing a Song of Sixpence,* Highland Music Company, 1988

Lebret, Elisabeth: *Pentatonic Songs,* Waldorf Association of Ontario, 1985

Nelson, Esther, L.: *Singing and Dancing Games for the Very Young,* Sterling Publishing Co. Inc., NY, 1982

Opie, Iona & Peter: *The Oxford Nursery Rhyme Book,* OUP, 1955

Opie, Iona & Peter: *The Puffin Book of Nursery Rhymes,* Penguin Books, 1963

Opie, Iona & Peter: *The Singing Game,* OUP, 1985

Opie, Iona & Peter: *The Oxford Book of Nursery Rhymes,* OUP, 1951

Polee, Mathilde and Rosenberg, Petra: *Lullaby Treasury,* Floris Books, 1997

Poulsson, Emilie: *Finger Plays for Nursery and Kindergarten,* Dover Publishing Inc., NY 1971

Roberts, Sheena: *Playsongs,* A & C Black, 2002

Shaw, Margaret Fay: *Folksongs and Folklore of South Uist,* Birlinn Ltd, Edinburgh, 1999

Swinger, Marlys: *Sing through the Day,* Plough Publishing House, NY, 1968

Swinger, Marlys: *Sing through the Seasons,* Plough Publishing House, NY, 1972

Music books: no author/editor cited

Strawberry Fair, A & C Black Ltd 1985

Spring Collection of Poems, Songs and Stories for young children, Wynstones Press, 1999

Summer Collection of Poems, Songs and Stories for young children, Wynstones Press, 1999

Autumn Collection of Poems, Songs and Stories for young children, Wynstones Press, 1999

Winter Collection of Poems, Songs and Stories for young children, Wynstones Press, 1999

Gateways: Poems, Songs and Stories for young children, Wynstones Press, 1999

Songs by Candy Verney

5 little mice	Hokey pokey whisky thum
At sunset / In the evening	How many days
Blow wind blow	My new little sister
Carrots, potatoes, and cabbage and peas	Praise be God for Mother Earth
Clap up high, clap down low	Ring the bell
Cobbler, cobbler	Shoe a little horse
Early in the morning	There was an old crow
Earth who gives to us our food	When I get up in the morning
Goodbye now	Which is the way to fairyland

All other songs in the book, except for those whose origins could not be traced, are either included in the publications listed or are in the public domain as well-known songs.

Books

Campbell, Patricia Shehan: *Songs in their Heads, music and its meaning in children's lives,* Oxford University Press 1998

Deliege: *Musical Beginnings,* Oxford University Press 1996

Griffiths, Jay: *Pip, Pip, A Sideways Look at Time,* Flamingo Press 1999

Katalin, Forrai: *Music in Preschool,* Corvina Press 1990

McClellan, Randall: *The Healing Power of Music,* Amity House NY 1988

Oldfield, Lynne: *Free To Learn,* Hawthorn Press 2001

Rawson, Martyn, and Rose, Michael: *Ready To Learn,* Hawthorn Press 2002

Sandor, Frigyes (ed.): *Music Education in Hungary,* Boosey & Hawkes and Corvina Press, 1975

Thomas, Heather: *Journey through time in Verse and Rhyme,* Rudolf Steiner Press 1987

Traherne, Thomas: *Selected Meditations,* Carcanet Press 1997

Book of a Thousand Poems, Collins Educational,1972 [no editor cited]

Articles

Deliege: 'Musical Beginnings', OUP, 1996

Goddard Blythe, Sally: 'Music and Movement – Are these the lost keys to early learning?' Paper presented at the 10th European Conference of Neuro-Development Delay in Children with Specific Learning Difficulties, Chester 6-8 March 1998

Heather, Simon: 'The Healing Power of Sound', *Positive Health,* May 2001

Papousek, H. and Papousek. M: 'Intuitive Parenting' in: Osovsky Wiley, J.D (ed.), *Handbook of Infant Development,* New York 1987

Lindenberg, Christof-Andreas: 'The Child and Hearing': 3 articles in *The Cresset,* Camphill Publication, Vol 17 nos.2, 3, 4: 1971

Websites

- Children's Music by Nancy Stewart, Animal Crackers/Friends Street Music, 6505 SE 28th Street, Mercer Island, WA 98040, USA, **www.nancymusic.com**

- School of Scottish Studies Archive, **www.pearl.arts.ed.ac.uk**

- Topic Records Ltd, The Voice of the People series, **www.topicrecords.co.uk**

- 'The Power of Music' – worldwide literature review of authoritative articles which address the power of music, **www.thepowerofmusic.co.uk**

- 'Wired for Sound: The Essential Connection between Music and Development' by Cynthia Ensign Baney, **www.gymboreeplayuk.com/CATresearch.htm**

- International Kodaly Society, **www.iks.hu**

- British Kodaly Academy, **www.britishkodalyacademy.org**

- Organization of American Kodaly Educators, **www.oake.org**

- Steiner Waldorf Schools Fellowship, **www.steinerwaldorf.org.uk**

Organisations

- Singing in the Round
  Candy Verney offers regular and one-off workshops for pre-school children, parents and teachers. Her other work includes the popular Singing in the Round community choirs in Bath and Wiltshire, weekend workshops that combine singing with Landscape and Art, and courses for Bild-Werk in Frauenau, Germany. She also helps organise 'Singing Round the Town', a unique annual summer community festival in Bradford on Avon.
  Tel: (++44) (0) 1225 867366 E-mail: candyverney@hotmail.com
  www.candyverney.co.uk
  www.singingintheround.co.uk

- The Natural Voice Practitioners' Network.
  An organisation for voice teachers sharing a common ethos and approach to voice and song work. 'We believe that singing is everyone's birthright and we are committed to teaching styles that are accepting and inclusive of all, regardless of musical experience and ability.' For information about: voice teachers; singing workshops; community choirs; recordings and song resources; voice events in your area, throughout the UK and beyond contact:
  www.naturalvoice.net

- The Voices Foundation
  Suite 2, Ground floor, 38 Ebury Street, London SW1 W OLU
  Tel: (++44) (0)20 7730 6677 E-mail: vf@voices.org.uk
  www.voices.org.uk

- The Listening Centre (Lewes) Ltd – Tomatis
  Maltings Studio, 16A Station Street, Lewes, East Sussex BN7 2DB
  Tel: (++44) (0)1273 474877 E-mail: enquiries@listeningcentre.co.uk
  www.listeningcentre.co.uk
  www.tomatis.com

- Caroline Price, Community Choir Leader
  Stream of Sound, 24 Cleveland Street, Stourbridge, West Midlands DY8 3UE
  Tel: (++44) (0)1384 377833
  www.streamofsound.co.uk

- Tonalis Music Centre
  4 Castle Farm Close, Leighterton, Gloucestershire GL8 8UY
  Tel/Fax: (++44) (0)1666 890460 E-mail: tonalis@aol.com
  Tonalis offers weekend workshops, courses and trainings in Music Education, Voicework and Community Musicing. Some of the themes which Tonalis works with are Children's Musical Development – a new developmental music curriculum, Teaching Music through Movement, Sharing Music – how social ideals can inspire music in schools and Newly Designed Instruments for meeting children's needs etc.
  www.tonalismusic.co.uk

Music index of first lines

Music index of first lines

125

CD track numbers – list of first lines

About the author

Candy Verney studied music at the University of Bristol, however most of her skills were learnt bringing up three sons and teaching music to all ages from the very young to the very old. She draws her inspiration from teaching methods used in Steiner/Waldorf education.

Candy currently teaches singing with parents and toddlers and leads adult community choirs in Bath, Wiltshire and further afield. She also works with companies and institutions, using singing as a tool for team-building and stress management. She firmly believes that, given sympathetic support, everyone can sing. She works individually with 'non-singers' and gains tremendous satisfaction from watching people grow in confidence as they find their voice.

Other books from Hawthorn Press

224pp; 250 x 200mm
paperback
978-1-869890-46-9

Festivals Together
Guide to multicultural celebration
Sue Fitzjohn, Minda Weston, Judy Large

This special book for families and teachers helps you celebrate festivals from cultures from all over the world. This resource guide for celebration introduces a selection of 26 Buddhist, Christian, Hindu, Jewish, Muslim and Sikh festivals. It offers a lively introduction to the wealth of different ways of life. There are stories, things to make, recipes, songs, customs and activities for each festival, comprehensively illustrated.

You will be able to share in the adventures of Anancy the spider trickster, how Ganesh got his elephant head and share in Eid, Holi, Wesak, Advent, Divali, Chinese New Year and more.

'The ideal book for anyone who wants to tackle multicultural festivals.'
Nursery World

224pp; 250 x 200mm
paperback
978-0-950706-23-8

Festivals, Family and Food
Guide to seasonal celebration
Diana Carey and Judy Large

This family favourite is a unique, well loved source of stories, recipes, things to make, activities, poems, songs and festivals. Each festival such as Christmas, Candlemas and Martinmas has its own, well illustrated chapter.

There are also sections on Birthdays, Rainy Days, Convalescence and a birthday Calendar. The perfect present for a family, it explores the numerous festivals that children love celebrating.

'It's an invaluable resource book'   *The Observer*

'Every family should have one'   *Daily Mail*

All Year Round
A Calendar of celebrations
Ann Druitt, Christine Fynes-Clinton, Marije Rowling

All Year Round is brimming with things to make; activities, stories, poems and songs to share with your family. It is full of well illustrated ideas for fun and celebration: from Candlemas to Christmas and Midsummer's day to the Winter solstice.

Observing the round of festivals is an enjoyable way to bring rhythm into children's lives and provide a series of meaningful landmarks to look forward to. Each festival has a special character of its own: participation can deepen our understanding and love of nature and bring a gift to the whole family.

320pp; 250 x 200mm; paperback; 978-1-869890-47-6

The Children's Year
Seasonal crafts and clothes
Stephanie Cooper, Christine Fynes-Clinton, Marije Rowling

You needn't be an experienced craftsperson to create beautiful things! This step by step, well illustrated book with clear instructions shows you how to get started. Children and parents are encouraged to try all sorts of handwork, with different projects relating to the seasons of the year.

Here are soft toys, wooden toys, moving toys such as balancing birds or climbing gnomes, horses, woolly hats, mobiles and dolls. Designs and patterns for children's clothing are included, using natural fabrics. Over 100 treasures to make, in seasonal groupings.

192pp; 250 x 200mm; paperback; 978-1-903458-59-4

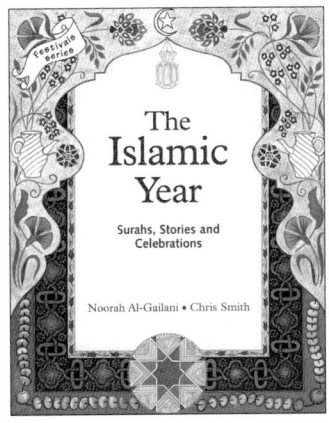

The Islamic Year
Surahs, Stories and Celebrations
Noorah Al-Gailani and Chris Smith

Celebrate the Islamic Year in your family or at school! You are invited to explore Muslim festivals with this inspiring treasury of stories, surahs, songs, games, recipes, craft and art activities. Folk tales illustrate the core values of Islamic culture with gentle humour and wisdom. *The Islamic Year* is beautifully illustrated with traditional patterns, maps and pictures drawn from many parts of the Muslim world, and Arabic calligraphy.

240pp; 250 x 200mm; paperback; 978-1-903458-14-3

Celebrating Irish Festivals
Calendar of seasonal celebrations
Ruth Marshall

If you are interested in Irish traditions, need a family or school resource, then here is an inspiring treasury of stories, beautiful illustrations, poems, traditions, food, activities, games, dances and songs. Reaching back to the ancient festivals of Imbolc, Bealtaine, Lughnasadh, Samhain, and to Celtic Christianity – Ruth Marshall also offers new ways for engaging children.

'A comprehensive calendar of festivals that children will cherish.'
Irelands Own, Summer 2003

224pp; 250 x 200mm; paperback; 978-1-903458-23-5

Celebrating Christmas Together

Nativity and Three Kings Plays with stories and songs

Estelle Bryer and Janni Nicol

Create the wonder of Christmas with your children at school or at home – starting with a simple Advent Calendar and Crib Scene. This Treasury includes the Nativity Play, with staging directions and instructions for simple costumes and props, plus songs and music to accompany the play.

'A practical and beautiful guide to making Christmas a magical time for children.'   Sally Jenkinson, author of *The Genius of Play*

96pp; 210 x 148mm; paperback; 978-1-903458-20-4

Christmas Stories Together

Estelle Bryer and Janni Nicol

Here is a treasure trove of 36 tales for children aged 3-9. The stories range from Advent through Christmas ending with the Holy Family's flight into Egypt – in fact, tales for the whole year. These stories will soon become family favourites, with their imaginative yet down to earth language and lively illustrations.

'This book is alight with the genius of storytelling. It tenderly shows how to weave a pattern of stories over Advent and the twelve days of Christmas.'
          Nancy Mellon, author of *Storytelling with Children*

128pp; 210 x 148mm; paperback; 978-1-903458-22-8

Games Children Play
How games and sport help children develop
Kim-John Payne
Illustrated by Marije Rowling

Games Children Play offers an accessible
guide to games with children of age three
upwards. These games are all tried and tested,
and are the basis for the author's extensive teacher
training work. The book explores children's personal development and how this is expressed
in movement, play, songs and games. Each game is clearly and simply described, with diagrams
or drawings, and accompanied by an explanation of why this game is helpful at a particular
age. The equipment that may be needed is basic, cheap and easily available.

192pp; 297 x 210mm; paperback; 978-1-869890-78-0

Making Waldorf Dolls
(Formerly 'Kinder Dolls')
Maricristin Sealey

A new edition of this family favourite, updated with a fully revised
resource list. This comprehensive, well illustrated book will give
even the most nervous beginner the confidence to produce a
unique, handcrafted toy from natural materials. Start with the
basic baby doll which gives you a good grounding in all the basics,
and then progress to a more ambitious limbed or jointed doll.
Making Waldorf Dolls includes instructions for 10 different dolls,
a wealth of ideas for hairstyles, lots of patterns for clothes and
accessories, and advice on tools, techniques and materials.

*'A valuable primer, full of practical tips, simple designs and clear, easy
to follow instructions.'*

Sara McDonald, Magic Cabin Dolls

160pp; 246 x 189mm; paperback; 978-1-903458-58-7

Pull the Other One!
String Games and Stories Book 1
Michael Taylor

This well-travelled and entertaining series of tales is accompanied by clear instructions and explanatory diagrams – guaranteed not to tie you in knots and will teach you tricks with which to dazzle your friends!

'A practical and entertaining guide, which pulls together a wealth of ideas from different cultures and revives a forgotten art. I think parents as well as children will enjoy this book.'

Sheila Munro, parenting author

128pp; 216 x 148mm; drawings; paperback; 978-1-869890-49-0

Now You See It...
String Games and Stories Book 2
Michael Taylor

String Games are fun, inviting children to exercise skill, imagination and teamwork. They give hands and fingers something clever and artistic to do! Following the success of *Pull the Other One!*, here are more of Michael Taylor's favourite string games, ideal for family travel, for creative play and for party tricks.

136pp; 216 x 148mm; paperback; 978-1-903458-21-1

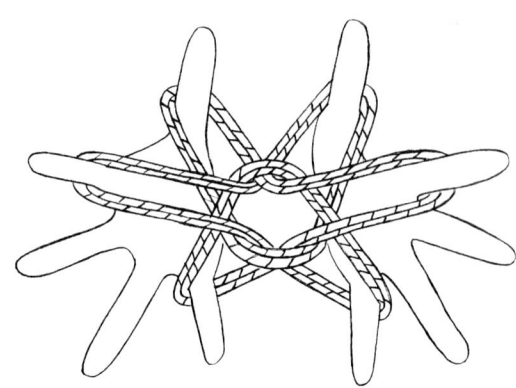

'Six-pointed star' from Book 1

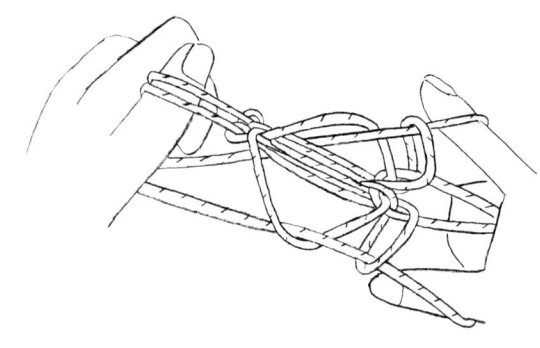

'The Frog' from Book 2

Storytelling with Children
Nancy Mellon

Telling stories awakens wonder and creates special occasions with children, whether it is bedtime, around the fire or on rainy days. Nancy Mellon shows how you can become a confident storyteller and enrich your family with the power of story.

'Nancy Mellon continues to be an inspiration for storytellers old and new. Her experience, advice and suggestions work wonders. They are potent seeds that give you the creative confidence to find your own style of storytelling.'
Ashley Ramsden, Director of the School of Storytelling, Emerson College

192pp; 216 x 138mm; paperback; 978-1-903458-08-2

Set Free Childhood
Parents' survival guide to coping with computers and TV
Martin Large

Children watch TV and use computers for five hours daily on average. The result? Record levels of learning difficulties, obesity, eating disorders, sleep problems, language delay, aggressive behaviour, anxiety – and children on fast forward. However, *Set Free Childhood* shows you how to counter screen culture and create a calmer, more enjoyable family life.

'TV programming is geared to hold children's attention, so that they find it hard to walk away. Children, therefore, need adults' help with switching off.'
The Independent

'A comprehensive, practical and readable guide … the skilful interplay between academic research and anecdotal evidence engages the reader.'
Jane Morris-Brown, *Steiner Education*

240pp; 216 x 138mm; paperback; 978-1-903458-43-3

Free Range Education

How home education works

Terri Dowty (ed)

Welcome to this essential handbook for families considering or starting out in home education. *Free Range Education* is full of family stories, resources, burning questions, humour, tips, practical steps and useful advice so you can choose what best suits your family situation. You are already your child's main teacher and these families show how home education can work for you. Both parents and children offer useful guidance, based on their experience.

Here are:

- practical answers to questions such as 'how do they socialise?', 'money?', 'how do they take exams?', 'what about time for yourself?';
- inspiring blow by blow accounts with stories from 'home education' graduates about their jobs, training and lives; resources, contacts, networks and websites where you can get support;
- a friendly overview of the legal position to help you deal constructively with education authorities and find the advice you need;
- … and cartoons about Educating Archie for light relief!

'Free Range Education *will encourage anyone contemplating the big step of going it alone…*'

Kids Out, August 2000

256pp; 210 x 148mm; paperback; 978-1-903458-07-5

For further information or a book catalogue, please contact:

Hawthorn Press, 1 Lansdown Lane, Stroud, Gloucestershire GL5 1BJ
Tel: (01453) 757040 Fax: (01453) 751138 E-mail: info@hawthornpress.com
Website: www.hawthornpress.com

If you have difficulties ordering Hawthorn Press books from a bookshop,
you can order direct from:

Booksource, 50 Cambuslang Road, Glasgow G32 8NB
Tel: (0845) 370 0063 Fax: (0845) 370 0064 E-mail: orders@booksource.net

or you can order online at **www.hawthornpress.com**

Dear Reader

If you wish to follow up your reading of this book, please tick the boxes below as appropriate, fill in your name and address and return to Hawthorn Press:

☐ Please send me a catalogue of other Hawthorn Press books.

☐ Please send me details of Festivals events and courses.

Questions I have about *Festivals* are:

Name _____

Address _____

_____

Postcode _____ Tel. no. _____

Please return to:

Hawthorn Press, 1 Lansdown Lane, Stroud, Gloucestershire. GL5 1BJ, UK
or Fax (01453) 751138

SD